C000254760

The Bible Hunter

The Bible Hunter

The Quest for the Original New Testament

Jürgen Gottschlich

Translated by John Brownjohn

Originally published in 2010 as *Der Bibeljaeger* by Christoph Links Verlag GmbH
Copyright © Christoph Links Verlag GmbH, 2010, 2013

Translation copyright © John Brownjohn, 2013
The moral right of the author has been asserted

First published in Great Britain in 2013 by
Haus Publishing Ltd
70 Cadogan Place
London SW1X 9AH
www.hauspublishing.com

A CIP record for this book is available from the British Library

Print ISBN: 978-1-908323-47-7
Ebook ISBN: 978-1-908323-48-4

Printed and bound in Great Britain by TJ International Ltd.

The translation of this work was supported by a grant from the Goethe-Institut,
which is funded by the German Ministry of Foreign Affairs.

GOETHE
INSTITUT

Contents

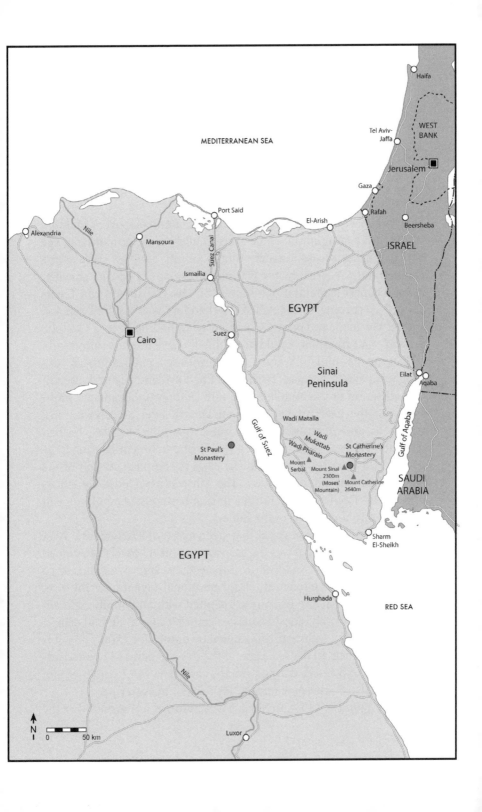

Foreword

It all began with a visit to an antique shop in Kadiköy, part of Istanbul. While rummaging among some dusty English- and German-language books, I came across a small volume simply entitled *Tischendorf-Erinnerungen*. Written by the German missionary Ludwig Schneller, it was a euphoric memoir of his father-in-law, Constantin von Tischendorf. According to Schneller, Tischendorf was a gifted scholar, a great German, and a true Christian who, had he been a Catholic instead of a Protestant, would undoubtedly have merited sainthood.

Despite its adulatory tone, this devotional publication of 1954 caught my fancy, because Tischendorf had evidently caused a scholarly sensation in the middle of the 19th century. In an ancient monastery in the heart of Egypt's Sinai Desert, after an adventurous, strenuous and not undangerous quest spanning decades, he had unearthed a stack of handwritten sheets of parchment bearing large parts of the Old Testament and the earliest complete version of the New Testament yet discovered. The 4th-century Codex Sinaiticus brought by Tischendorf to Europe in 1859 represented a milestone in research into the origins of the Bible.

Despite this, I had never at that stage heard of Tischendorf. Who was this man, and what was the relevance of his discovery? Intrigued by his personality, I resolved to pursue those questions and, in so doing, underwent an intellectual and emotional adventure of my own. I travelled to Sinai and became acquainted with an entirely different world in one of the oldest monasteries in existence: St Catherine's, which has been continuously occupied by monks for 1,500 years. It is a world in which, in the seclusion of the desert, men still live according to rules and rituals dating from the early days of Christianity, and which still harbours some immensely ancient manuscripts.

I soon found out that, in Sinai, Tischendorf is not regarded as the luminary described by his son-in-law Ludwig Schneller – far from it. To the monks, he is the man who purloined their most precious manuscript – who lent it to the Tsarist court in St Petersburg but never returned it.

Subsequently sold to the British by Stalin, the Codex Sinaiticus is now one of the showpieces of the British Library. This makes it one of the series of ancient works of art whose return from the inventories of European and American museums is being more and more vehemently demanded by their countries of origin. Art theft or the conservation of unique cultural assets? Even if that question is not always easy to decide, in the cases of the Codex Sinaiticus, the famous bust of Nefertiti, and the Parthenon frieze from the Athenian Acropolis, Egypt and Greece want their treasures back just like the monks of St Catherine's in the Sinai Desert. Modern research has confirmed that the Codex Sinaiticus was written around AD 350, possibly even at the behest of the celebrated Emperor Constantine, who granted privileges to the Christian sect, hitherto proscribed and persecuted throughout the Roman Empire, and thus paved the way for Christianity to become a world religion.

But the Codex Sinaiticus – Constantine's Bible – contains parts of the New Testament for which one would look in vain today. These were weeded out later, on the way to its final form. The Book of Books is not an integrated whole. The Codex exemplifies this with particular clarity, because it was repeatedly amended in ways that clearly indicate the prevailing state of theological thought. The Christians' sacred book took several centuries to develop into its current form. When Enlightenment took effect in theology as well as science at the beginning of the 19th century and the Bible, too, was submitted to critical examination, it soon emerged that the origins of the New Testament are complex and have still to be fully explored. To Tischendorf, however, casting doubt on the Bible was sheer blasphemy. In order to silence the critics, he aspired to rediscover the original text of the New Testament, the lost Word, and lend it fresh validity.

Tischendorf was positively obsessed with this mission. His personal papers, which I have been privileged to examine in Leipzig University Library, enable one to reconstruct a life in which his family, but also his Leipzig University colleagues, were wholly subordinate to his ambition and his grand aim in life. In order to fulfil his mission, he sought and found support from fundamentalist clergy and the most reactionary monarchy in Europe, the Russian imperial court. Years of self-sacrificial work enabled him to decipher ancient Greek manuscripts that had defeated all his predecessors. Although vain, he wholeheartedly devoted his life to his mission.

Politically, Tischendorf was conservative to the core. He fought against Enlightenment and against the republican movement in Germany. He was a member of the worldwide 'Evangelical Alliance' founded in 1846, an association of Protestant churches opposed to questioning the Bible and increasing secularization. Theologically and politically, therefore, Tischendorf was among the forerunners of today's evangelical movement.

The Codex Sinaiticus, which he discovered in St Catherine's Monastery in the Sinai Desert and, by so doing, may well have preserved from gradual disintegration, has since become the subject of a unique scientific pilot project. In 2001, in order to reunite the parchment leaves of the Codex, which are now divided between London, Leipzig, St Petersburg and the Sinai monastery, the British Library launched a scheme to install one of the world's oldest books on the Internet. In 2005, after a great deal of diplomatic spadework, the digitization and transcription of the Codex began. In 2009, on the occasion of a major international conference in London, the start button was pressed. The oldest Bible in the world was on the net, but the servers crashed within minutes because millions of people wanted to access its pages. These problems have since been eliminated. On www.codexsinaiticus.net, anyone can now view what others spent a lifetime fighting for.

The Desert Monastery

A long journey to the monks of the Sinai Desert

Cairo

It's two in the morning. Old Cairo Airport, inhospitable enough by day, is almost deserted at this hour. A few dilapidated benches are all the arrivals hall has to offer. Only a handful of taxi drivers and a few tourist touts are standing their ground – more from habit, one suspects, than in the hope of doing any business. Once the last plane has landed and the passengers have been released into the Cairo night, the lights in the arrivals hall go out. Being unable to check into my hotel until midday, I had really wanted to spend a few hours in an airport café before driving into the city by the light of the rising sun, but no such luck. There are few things more unpleasant than having to set off for an unfamiliar city in an unfamiliar country in the middle of the night, especially when that city is located on an unfamiliar continent and you're unacquainted with local customs. Involuntarily, you wonder if your taxi driver is a genuine taxi driver, or if your journey will end in the darkness of some Egyptian slum.

Such are the fears conjured up by an urban Moloch, a seething chaos by day that easily becomes a nightmare after dark, with its bewildering alternation of motor roads and narrow, unlit alleyways. Cairo, heart of the Muslim world, is more of an aggregate than a comprehensible metropolis, and designed to thoroughly bewilder a European. And I haven't just come from the orderly tedium of Stuttgart or Hanover, but from Istanbul, itself a metropolis of 15 million predominantly Muslim inhabitants, though one that resembles a model West European community compared to Cairo. Minarets glide dimly past the taxi's windows, dilapidated tenement buildings alternate with

A 19th-century photograph of St Catherine's Monastery in the mountainous isolation of southern Sinai. The foot of Mount Sinai can be seen on the left.

once-magical oriental palaces whose heyday is long past. The cabby has only a rough idea of the location of the hotel whose address I handed him on a slip of paper. He keeps stopping to enquire the way from shady-looking characters loitering outside the last open cafés. Still, it really does look as if he means to deliver me to the address in question.

Two hours later, when we actually pull up outside the building of which my Cairo hotel occupies the top two floors, I'm so relieved that I promptly hand over a grossly exorbitant sum of money – how exorbitant, I learn only later. Never mind, though, what matters is, I can take refuge in an armchair in the lobby, where I safely doze away the remaining hours of the night. A little while later, when the sun rises in a flawlessly blue sky, its rays illuminate a city unlike any other in the world. Cairo is an old city, at least compared to most other human settlements, even though it is one of the very youngest in Egyptian history. Founded by the Abbasid dynasty in around 700 BC, Cairo, or, as it was then, El Qahira, cannot match the 4,600 years for which the Pyramids of Giza have now been standing. It has, however, undergone sundry transformations in its 1,300 years of existence. It took 500 years for the tented city of the Islamic conquerors who captured Byzantine Alexandria in 641 and wrested control of Egypt from the East Roman Empire to develop into a metropolis that could hold its own against Baghdad and Damascus. Power on the Nile was then assumed by Saladin, the famous military leader who drove the Crusaders from Jerusalem. Under his rule the population of the city grew to over 120,000 inhabitants. But the last and most far-reaching change began in the 1930s. Because of population growth in the villages bordering the Nile, fewer and fewer people could live off their agricultural produce. Consequently, they sought salvation in the metropolis, and Cairo became positively inundated with people.

Now that Greater Cairo boasts some 30 million inhabitants, over a third of Egypt's entire population lives in the capital's catchment area. This makes the metropolis on the Nile probably the biggest conurbation in the African continent. Most Cairenes live in appalling conditions, in overcrowded, utterly squalid housing. In many parts of the city one is instantly reminded of reports that whole buildings have collapsed without warning because unscrupulous developers economized on cement. What strikes one most of all, however, is the ubiquitous greyish-brown dust. Every building, every tree and bush is coated with a grey film which Cairo's rare showers of rain fail to rinse off. The metropolis on the Nile is a city in a desert, and the wind keeps blowing the desert into the city.

It isn't easy to find your way around Cairo, even in daytime. The place is vast, in fact the city centre alone covers 400 square kilometres and has been expanding without any discernible plan for the past century. I have made a 10.00 a.m. appointment with the vicar of the Sinaite monks at their Cairo monastery, hoping that he will grant me access to St Catherine's, the ancient monastery in the Sinai Desert. The first hermits are said to have appeared in that desert, there to spend their lives in accordance with God's will, only 180 years after the birth of Christ.

Father Aaron, the Cairo face of the Sinai monks, is an impressive figure. Tall and white-haired, with a contrasting pair of black horn-rimmed glasses, he represents his monastery's interests in the capital. The Sinaites' Cairo outpost may once have been an imposing residence on the outskirts of the city, but it has long since been engulfed by the urban Moloch and now stands on a noisy, traffic-infested square whose most noticeable feature is a car showroom opposite the monastery. A big building, the monastery itself is showing its age and needs extensive renovation. The garden gate is open, and some Arab employees' children are playing on the parched grass inside. A little girl offers to show me the way, but the whole building seems deserted. She conducts me into a small kitchen, evidently assuming that some grown-up members of the household will be there, but this is a misconception. We trail along some more passages until we hear a loud voice issuing from an open door at the far end. Seated at a big desk, Father Aaron is on the phone – clearly on a very poor line. He beckons me in, hangs up in annoyance, and scrutinizes me closely.

Father Aaron has spent 40 years of his life in the seclusion of the Sinai monastery, but betweentimes, in the 1960s, he spent several years in Germany. His German is somewhat rusty but impeccable in other respects. His memories of Germany are predominantly pleasant, which is fortunate, as that is bound to favour my plans. Our only contact hitherto has been three phone calls, and Father Aaron tends to be terse on the phone, but now, face to face, he starts chatting. Happy to be able to reminisce about his experiences in Germany, he remembers Berlin as a divided city and says how much he liked Hamburg. I finally succeed in broaching the reason for my presence. Yes, he will notify Sinai of my visit. Even Germany's Chancellor and Federal President visited St Catherine's in the days when Sinai was under Israeli occupation – then one could fly from Tel Aviv to a military airfield not far from the monastery. This is no longer possible, alas, and getting there has become more difficult again. He tries at once to get through to Father Gabriel, who is evidently the desert monks' quartermaster, but the line remains dead. Telecom Egypt, as I have already had occasion to note, still falls far short of what is technologically feasible.

'Oh, so you're interested in Tischendorf!'

My trip to Sinai was preceded by lengthy and fruitless attempts to get in touch with the desert monastery by phone, email, and even, quite conventionally, by post. Yet I thought I'd gone about my plan in a clever manner. Having been a longtime correspondent in Istanbul, I was acquainted with Patriarch Bartholomew, Greek Orthodox patriarch of Constantinople – as the Orthodox Church persists in calling Istanbul – and spiritual head of the Orthodox Church as a whole. The spokesman of the patriarchate, Father Dositheos, has spent a long time in Germany, like his brother Aaron in Cairo, so German correspondents can gain access to him with relative ease.

But conditions within the Orthodox Church are complicated. Although Dositheos did not reject my request that he put me in touch with the Sinaite brothers, or, better still, write me a letter of recommendation to the monks of St Catherine's, it developed into a waiting game. The main reason, I grasped only later, was a name: Constantin von Tischendorf. After all, my aim in going to Sinai was to follow in the footsteps of a man of the 19th century: the German theologian, palaeographer and adventurer who paid several visits to the monastery between 1844 and 1859, leaving behind a lasting impression and a deep-seated feeling of resentment. Tischendorf had been on a quest, though not for any spiritual encounters with God; he was not searching the solitude of the desert in the hope of deepening his religious convictions – no, he was seeking the origins of the Bible. Subsequently ennobled by the Tsar of Russia, he was seeking the truth about Jesus Christ, not in prayer but in black on white – or, rather, brown on yellow, as writing on papyrus or parchment appears. A hunter in search of a long-lost treasure, he hoped to find the origins of Christianity in Sinai, of all places: an area that had belonged to the Islamic world for a thousand years or more.

Mention of Tischendorf would evoke a wide variety of reactions in the ensuing months of my quest. Father Dositheos left it at a brief exclamation: 'Oh, so you're interested in Tischendorf!' Quickly changing the subject, we spoke of the problems affecting the Greek Orthodox ecumenical patriarchate in Turkey. That the head of the Orthodox Church should still reside in Istanbul seems at first sight as incongruous as if the Vatican were installed in a Buddhist country. On the other hand, the Orthodox Church thinks in centuries, not years or decades. Even though the Ottomans captured Constantinople in 1453 and the capital of Christian Byzantium transformed itself into that of the Islamic Ottoman Empire, the Greek Orthodox Church still thinks of the city as Constantinople, the place where Christianity became the state religion and, thus, the immutable seat of the supreme pastor of the only true church.

But otherwise than in the Catholic Church, the Patriarch of Constantinople is *primus inter pares,* first among equals and not the head of a world church. The individual Orthodox churches in Greece, Russia, Serbia, Bulgaria, Palestine, and other countries are autocephalous churches that all elect their own patriarchs. Since the end of the Communist era in Russia and the Balkans, these have once more wielded considerable power and perceptible influence. In comparison with Cyril I, the patriarch of Russia, who presides over some 100 million believers, Bartholomew, the current ecumenical patriarch, is a king without a country. The Turkish government recognizes him only as spiritual head of Istanbul's last 3,000 Greeks, and even counting the Aegean Islands and the monasteries on Mount Athos, which are subject to his episcopal jurisdiction, his flock numbers barely 10,000 sheep. Any question affecting another Orthodox Church is a delicate diplomatic matter, which is why those at the seat of the Constantinople patriarchate think twice before becoming involved. Consequently, the patriarchate's spokesman dismissed me with a vague undertaking to attend to my request. Weeks later I received the terse information that visitors to the monastery did not require a recommendation from the Constantinople patriarchate. Instead, I should apply direct to the head of the autonomous Orthodox Church of Sinai, His Holiness Archbishop Damianos, Cairo address herewith. After a few more weeks, when my letter had elicited no response, I tried telephoning. One morning, after several attempts, someone actually came on the line. It was Father Aaron, but all he could tell me was that all correspondence was forwarded to the monastery, and I should call there direct. Being acquainted with the state of the Egyptian telephone lines in the desert, however, he had a tip for me that eventually bore fruit: the mobile number of the monastery's second-in-command, Father Ionnides, who could usually, he said, be reached in the evenings.

Several evenings went by before a voice in the desert replied. However, my mention of Constantin von Tischendorf made Father Ionnides equally loath to issue me with an invitation to the monastery. First, he said, I must contact Archbishop Damianos. He gave me another phone number, adding, 'Call the archbishop right away – he's in his study.' But the said number only emitted suspicious noises like those familiar to me from my numerous previous attempts in Cairo. I didn't get through until I had queried Father Ionnides again and been given yet another number to try. His Holiness Samartsis Damianos, 75 years old and elected head of the autonomous archdiocese of Sinai for the past 35, answered the phone. I was so surprised, it took me a few seconds to introduce myself and present my request. 'Ah, a book about Tischendorf,' said Damianos after another alarmingly long pause. 'That's a delicate matter.' I gathered from him that the monastery was engaged in preparing a publication of its own on that 'delicate matter', so it could not at present – 'everything is still up in the air, my son' – grant me access to any hitherto unpublished documents. That wouldn't be necessary, I explained hurriedly; I was a journalist, not a scholar. I was more interested in gaining a general impression of life in the monastery, in what the monks had heard tell of 'the German treasure hunter', and in their legendary library.

7

After asking some more personal questions, Archbishop Damianos confronted me with a practical objection: Father Justin, the monastery's librarian and a Tischendorf expert, was leaving for the United States in a few days' time and would be gone for two months. That sounded like a knockout blow. It only remained for me to ask, rather feebly, if it would be possible to confer with him and the archbishop beforehand. After another ominous silence I heard the unexpected question: 'Can you get here within the week?' I said yes at once and expressed myself duly grateful. 'Don't thank me too soon,' was the only response, and that concluded the conversation.

And that was how, a few days later, I came to be seated in front of Father Aaron's desk in Cairo, receiving last-minute instructions for my trip to the desert. In his spiky, upright hand, the monk wrote the following on a slip of paper: 'Abbasseya bus station, Sinai terminal, 10.00 a.m. tomorrow.'

The journey

The Sinai Peninsula, whose apex protrudes into the Red Sea, being bounded on the west by the Gulf of Suez and on the east by the Gulf of Aqaba, forms a natural geological buffer between Africa, the southern shore of the Mediterranean, and the Arabian subcontinent. The pharaohs were obliged to send their armies across the Sinai Desert on all their forays into Palestine and Mesopotamia. That was why they opened up the dry, rocky, and, in the south, mountainous peninsula at an early stage and built the requisite transport routes. However, the armies' route ran along the Mediterranean, exactly like those used by caravans. The inhospitable south of the peninsula was opened up to only a minor extent because of its minerals. The rulers of pharaonic Egypt dug for precious stones there from the very earliest times. Even today, mines 4,000 years old yield the blue turquoises for which Sinai is famed. The further south one goes, the higher the mountains become. Although northern Sinai is traversed by two big motor roads, the south has nothing but the coast road leading from Suez, via the new tourist centres around Sharm el-Sheikh, to the Israeli frontier. Branching off this coast road at a few points are secondary roads that lead into the interior along dry river beds between the mountains. One of these is the Wadi Pharain, a sort of cul-de-sac, at the end of which stands St Catherine's Monastery.

To allow for all eventualities, I got to Abbasseya bus station in good time and had ample opportunity to watch what went on there before my 'East Delta Travel' bus finally pulled in. Discounting the police checks at its entrance, the terminal was a tranquil little place by Cairo standards. A bus drove up only every half-hour, people leisurely stowed away the treasures they had acquired in the capital, and they seemed largely relaxed and happy to be setting off on the homeward trip to their villages. The only thing was, the buses were in a deplorable condition. The windows in our own vehicle were so dirty, I feared I wouldn't see a thing all the way, but my fellow passengers were unworried by either the lack of a view or the dilapidated seats, and I doubted if they wasted any thought on the probability that the brakes were no better than the rest of the vehicle. Who cared, though? There was no alternative in any case, and the mood aboard was good.

The bus was only moderately full to start with, but on the outskirts we took on a whole load of soldiers returning to their units. Sinai is still heavily militarized despite the peace treaty with Israel. Israeli troops conquered the whole of the peninsula during the Six Day War in 1967, only stopping short at Suez. Sinai remained Israeli until 1982, and Israeli troops did not begin their gradual withdrawal until after the Camp David Agreement of 1978.[1] The Egyptian army moved back into its positions and has remained there until now. The bus had to pass at least ten army checkpoints on the way to St Catherine's Monastery.

Cairo has no city limits in the conventional sense; it gradually peters out into desert. Once you're past the last outlying hovels, all that can be seen beside the motorway to Suez is a dusty, stony wasteland. The wilderness that stretches away to the horizon has nothing in common with the great, fascinating sandy deserts of North Africa and is simply an interminable expanse of stony ground across which the wind propels occasional clumps of thistly vegetation. The view remains just as dismal when the outskirts of Suez appear. Internationally known because it lent its name to the famous canal that links the Red Sea and the Mediterranean, thereby absolving ships from having to round the Cape of Good Hope, the town is little more than a collection of run-down blocks of flats, not a place that invites you to linger. The canal itself is a genuine disappointment because you don't see it at all. The road from Africa to Asia runs through a tunnel beneath it, and the route is flanked, a good kilometre before the entrance, by high embankments. The tunnel is heavily defended. The embankments have soldiers stationed on them every 20 metres and are interspersed with fortified machine-gun nests. The same scene presents itself when you emerge from the tunnel: high embankments and lots of soldiers but no Suez Canal. The road runs due south into the interior for the first 50 kilometres, so the sea is equally invisible at first. The Egyptians have made sundry attempts to green the stony desert beside the road. Water is conveyed to the Sinai Peninsula with the aid of a pipeline running beneath the Suez Canal from the Nile. This not only supplies the booming tourist towns on the Gulf of Aqaba and the remote St Catherine's Monastery but suffices to irrigate a few plantations as well. Although they don't yield much in the way of agricultural produce, the sporadic green expanses are a boon to the eye.

In general, however, the next 200 kilometres were pretty monotonous. Although there was an occasional glint of sea on the right-hand side, the view to our left was dominated by parched, stony desert. All that relieved the monotony was the sight of the offshore drilling rigs that enable the Egyptians to meet at least part of their demand for oil. Bare mountains loomed up gradually in the distance, drawing steadily nearer the sea. Nothing could now be heard in the bus but snatches of subdued conversation. It was some time since the driver had inserted another music cassette, and many of the passengers were dozing or asleep. Although it had been pretty cloudy all day, the mountains now glowed red in the setting sun. It was 4.30 p.m., and the bus had still to turn off up the Wadi Pharain. I was beginning to wonder how I would get into the monastery after dark, when the monks had retired for the night.

I knew from photographs that St Catherine's was enclosed by a high, fortresslike wall. In the old days, I had read, visitors were hoisted up the wall in a basket and admitted to the interior through a narrow aperture ten metres from the ground. Although there was now said to be an entrance at ground level, it would probably be shut long before I got there. Meanwhile, the bus had reached the mouth of the *wadi* and the most interesting part of the journey was beginning. Situated halfway between the sea and the monastery is the Pharain Oasis, which lends its name to the entire *wadi*. This oasis is the only place in southern Sinai with enough water to enable a vast grove of palm trees to flourish. Our bus reached the oasis just before sunset. The view was magnificent. The road was suddenly flanked for several kilometres by tall date palms – an almost incredible sight after all that stony desert all day long. What now looks sensational even to passengers on board a bus must have seemed well-nigh miraculous to the travellers of earlier times. The melodious sound of the word oasis becomes sensually perceptible here.

Most biblical scholars assume that if the tribes of Israel lingered anywhere on their long trek from Egypt to the Promised Land, it was here at this oasis. Even 3,500 years ago, there was not enough water 60 kilometres away on Mount Sinai to supply a substantial number of people for weeks or even months. The second book of the Old Testament recounts the story of this exodus. Instead of sending his people the easy way along the Mediterranean coast, Yahweh directed them to take the difficult, circuitous route through the Sinai Desert to the Promised Land, allegedly because he was afraid the Israelites might feel inclined to return to Egypt when confronted by the well-armed tribes along the shores of the Mediterranean. The highlight of this trek, which is supposed to have taken 40 years, was Moses' reception of the Ten Commandments on Mount Sinai, known in the Old Testament as Mount Horeb and identical with today's 2,300-metre-high Jebel Musa, or Mount Moses. Here in the midst of the southern Sinai Desert, in ancient terms several days' march from the shores of the Red Sea, God spoke to Moses from out of the burning bush at the foot of the mountain, and this was where Moses later climbed it to receive God's laws from out of the cloud.

Today, the Greek Orthodox St Catherine's Monastery stands precisely where Moses is said to have come upon the burning bush in 1300 BC – not only in the midst of the desert but, ever since the Muslim Arabs' conquest of Sinai around AD 650, in the midst of the Muslim world as well.

It really was dark by the time we reached our destination. Before the bus headed for its terminus in the village, it made one more stop at a major intersection. On one side lay a holiday complex; visible in our headlights on the other side was a signpost reading 'Katherin Monastery'. I had received some helpful information during the trip from two men seated across the aisle. They now gathered up their possessions and got out too, but my hopes that they might be also making for the monastery were soon dashed: they had booked into the holiday complex and were expected there. For all that, I was not alone. A figure of striking appearance also got out with us: a tall man in a black, hooded robe, he had caught my eye back at the bus station in Cairo. He was already seated aboard the bus when it arrived, but quite far back, so I had almost forgotten about him in the meantime. He could only be a Coptic priest, a member of Egypt's largest Christian minority.

The Copts

Copts, who constitute approximately ten per cent of the Egyptian population, are the largest Christian minority in a country of Islamic complexion. Churches can often be seen in Cairo in addition to its many mosques, and the small district known as Old Cairo resembles a Coptic open-air museum. It is a tiny quarter centred on an erstwhile Roman fortress known as Fort Babylon, which formed part of the Byzantine fortifications. When it was captured by Islamic troops in 640, there were more than 20 churches within its walls, several of which are still in existence today. Among them is Cairo's most famous and beautiful Coptic church, the Hanging Church (al-Mu'allaqa), so called because it is partly superimposed on the walls of the fortress. Dedicated to the Virgin Mary, it makes a very inviting impression and is a wonderful example of an ancient oriental church. The iconostasis, or screen bearing icons that separates the chancel from the nave in Greek Orthodox churches, consists entirely of warm-toned wood beautifully inlaid with mother-of-pearl.

Much controversy surrounds the true status of the Copts in Egypt. Do they enjoy equal rights with the Islamic majority, for instance, or are they thoroughly discriminated against and treated like second-class citizens? They do, in fact, have to contend with all the difficulties that confront minorities in most other countries, but the degree of oppression naturally depends on the prevailing situation and actual political system. Muhammad Hosni Mubarak, who ruled Egypt for decades with an iron fist, protected the minority, at least officially, and proclaimed the Coptic Christmas on 7 January a national holiday. On the other hand, he often failed to prevent rioting against the Copts, and their current situation is very much more difficult. It has been very rare for a Copt to get ahead in politics or public service. One of the few exceptions in this respect was the former UN Secretary-General, Boutros Boutros-Ghali.

Quite recently, after a long phase of restoration, a museum that impressively conveys the Copts' culture and religious history was reopened in the immediate neighbourhood of the Hanging Church. The Copts regard themselves as something akin to the last indigenous inhabitants of Egypt, who trace their language back to ancient Egyptian hieroglyphs and have not adopted the religion of the Islamic conquerors. Once upon a time, during the first 300 years AD, Alexandria was the greatest imperial city after Rome and the most important and influential place in early Christendom. The community of Alexandria traces its origins back to the apostle Mark, allegedly the author of the gospel that bears his name, who is said to have lived there until the year 68 and to have been its first bishop. The Coptic Church still invokes this direct line of succession and describes its present head, Pope Theodoros II, as Mark's 118th successor.

In 451, during the Council of Chalcedon, Alexandria seceded from the Orthodox Church and formed the Coptic Church.[2] What remained in Alexandria was a small Christian community that stayed true to Byzantium and within the Greek Orthodox rite. The monks of Sinai belonged and still belong to that community, hence my surprise that a Coptic priest should also be on his way to a Greek Orthodox monastery, but it was a fact: whether on a diplomatic mission or for personal reasons, the priest was going my way. We had plodded along in the dark for a few hundred metres when a big Toyota Land Cruiser came towards us and pulled up right alongside. It was full of monks on their way to the neighbouring village. The driver, who later turned out to be the Father Gabriel whom Father Aaron had vainly tried to

The Hanging Church in the old quarter of Cairo.

call in my presence, told the Copt that they would be back from the village in a few minutes' time and would then give us a lift to the monastery. If this wasn't a sign from heaven, it was at least a remarkable stroke of luck.

Instead of standing vainly outside the locked monastery in deepest darkness, we were driven right up to the gate by St Catherine's quartermaster and passed through the dimly lit, catacomblike entrance into the interior of the high-walled monastic fortress. Father Gabriel didn't ask who I was until we were inside the courtyard. I launched into a lengthy explanation. 'I have an appointment with the archbishop tomorrow morning,' I began, but that was enough. He handed me over to a young Arab who showed me to my room and conjured up a plate of cold spaghetti as well. The monastery was already in darkness, electric lights being visible in only a few windows. 'Early Mass starts at four, visitors come at six,' said my guide. Then I was on my own.

I could hardly take it in. So recently in Istanbul, I suddenly found myself in a completely different world, a 1,500-year-old monastery in the middle of the desert. As for the Coptic priest who had provided me with an entrée to St Catherine's, I never set eyes on him again in the five ensuing days I spent there.

Constantine the Founder

The Christian Church in the Roman Empire and the origins of the Bible

Anyone strolling through the old quarter of Istanbul from Hagia Sophia, once the largest church in Christendom, to the Grand Bazaar, will pass a column to which very few visitors pay much attention. In Turkish this monument is known as Cemberlitas, or 'hooped stone', because the column was reinforced with several iron bands under the Ottomans to prevent it from collapsing. Only recently restored, it spent years beneath an ugly sheet metal sheath that rendered it even less conspicuous. I myself had walked past the monument almost unheeding for nearly ten years until I was invited to ascend the column with a photographer friend who had been commissioned to photograph it for a report on the mysteries of Istanbul. This is normally impossible because the 35-metre Byzantine artefact is inaccessible, but the restorers' scaffolding enabled us to reach the top and view the historic Old City from an entirely new perspective.

Originally, I learnt, the column had supported a statue of the Roman Emperor Constantine the Great, who made Byzantium his capital in the year 330 and renamed it Constantinople. Constantine's statue once stood on top of the column, erect and divinely naked, with a spear in one hand and the imperial sceptre in the other. His head was encircled by an aureole and his gaze directed at the Hippodrome, where Hagia Sophia now stands.

Flanked by two marble colonnades, each two storeys high, the emperor's statue stood precisely in the middle of the Forum, at that time the new capital's central square. The 35-metre column consists of porphyry, the imperial stone, and is one of Istanbul's last surviving relics dating from the foundation of Constantinople. Constantine, who styled himself the first Christian emperor of Rome, had aroused my interest for some time; I had, after all, been living in his city for years, but more immediate problems had always prevented me from devoting greater attention to his person and the traces he left behind. This did not change until I started researching Constantin Tischendorf. Constantine is, after all, one of the key figures in early Christianity – indeed, some historians are convinced, and with good reason, that the modern Christian church owes its existence to him, and that without his intervention the early Christian community would have remained just one sect among the many other cults in the Roman Empire – a sect that would long ago have disappeared.[1] But there is more to it than that. A mysterious link exists between Constantine the Great and the monastery in the Sinai Desert. That link is the original text of the New Testament.

One of the best places to learn more about Constantine and his city is the Istanbul department of the German Archaeological Institute. Housed in a side wing of the consulate, a monumental Wilhelmine pile built at the end of the 19th century as the German Embassy in the capital of the Ottoman Empire, the Institute contains numerous treasures connected with the history of the city and its founder.

One of the Institute's former directors, Wolfgang Müller-Wiener, conducted extensive research into the city's history. Thanks to his archaeological studies we know what the most important features of Constantine's gigantic building project originally looked like. We know where the Forum was, and the Hippodrome, and the earliest parts of the imperial palace, and the city's principal church, the Church of the Holy Apostles, which also contained the mausoleum in which Constantine was buried. In addition to notes on the stone relics of the founder of Constantinople, the Institute's library contains a number of works that seek to explore the character of this scintillating but highly controversial personality of the ancient world.

Although subsequent Christian biographers, foremost among them his court scribe, Bishop Eusebius, took great pains to paint Constantine's career in the rosiest hue, it cannot be ignored that the emperor's conduct conflicted with Christian ideals in almost every respect. Constantine was an unscrupulous despot who unhesitatingly killed to attain his ends, and not only on the battlefield. He ordered the murder of all who seemed a threat to his ambitions, not excluding his wife and his eldest son.

Published in 2006, a biography of the emperor by Hartwin Brandt, Professor of Ancient History at Bamberg University, summarizes the present state of research into Constantine and essays a modern interpretation of the Christian Church's trailblazer.[2] Unlike his early Christian apologists, this portrays Constantine as a typical product of the Roman military aristocracy. His father was one of four reigning Augusti/Caesars; in violation of the rules of the reigning tetrarchy, he had himself proclaimed the new Caesar by his soldiers in a coup d'état, attacked all his coregents in turn and eliminated them in a violent military campaign, destroyed the tetrarchic system, and, after decades of incessant bloodshed, proclaimed himself sole ruler. His purported Christian awakening occurred in the course of this military campaign. On the eve of the battle against his rival Maxentius, who controlled Italy and the Roman capital, Constantine is said to have seen a fiery cross above the setting sun and, by way of explanation, the words *In Hoc Signo Vinces*, 'With this sign you will conquer'. God then appeared to him during the night before the decisive battle and bade him emblazon all his soldiers' shields with a representation of the symbol.

Constantine did, in fact, defeat Maxentius the following day at the famous Battle of the Milvian Bridge – less with God's help, to be honest, than because of his enemy's stupidity in leaving the safety of the walls of Rome to attack Constantine personally with his Praetorian Guard. Maxentius met his end in a thoroughly banal manner, drowning in the Tiber when pushed off the bridge by his own troops, who were already defeated and fleeing in panic. Constantine marched into Rome victorious, having sustained few casualties. In retrospect, this victory is associated with Christianity's breakthrough, for without it the Christian god would have stood no chance against the Roman pantheon. Had Constantine's troops lost the battle, he would probably have regarded the Christian sect's deity as an unreliable ally and promptly abandoned him.

Our mental image of Constantine is coloured by fragments of a 15-metre colossal statue from the Basilica of Constantine, whose head has survived intact.[3] It shows us the grim, coarse-featured countenance of a man whom it is hard to imagine deciding, after undergoing a religious awakening, to follow a god whose son preached turning the other cheek instead of smiting the smiter. All we know of Constantine suggests that he was an incredibly cool-headed seeker after power, and not given to high-flown enthusiasms. Nevertheless, he did display a definite preference for the Christian cult after his victory in Rome. As emperor of Western Rome – the Balkans and the Asiatic provinces were still under the control of his rivals Licinius and Maximinus Daia – he set administrative examples by exempting Christian priests from taxes and other public obligations and also decreed that ecclesiastical property expropriated during the years of persecution be returned.

Christianity in the Roman Empire

Even if we assume that Constantine's religious awakening is a legend subsequently purveyed by Christian biographers, a question remains: What prompted his soldiers to support a religion at first sight so incompatible with him and the martial traditions of Rome? Christianity had been spreading within the Roman Empire for about 200 years. Thanks to Paul, the earliest Judaeo-Christian communities in Palestine had developed into a religious movement represented mainly in the big cities of the Roman Empire, its lingua franca being Greek. The largest Christian centres in Constantine's day were in the cosmopolitan cities of the Roman East. Alexandria in Egypt, then the second-largest city after Rome, probably had the biggest Christian population, closely followed by Antioch in Syria, Caesarea in Palestine, and Ephesus and Miletus on the Aegean coast. Christianity was also very successful in North Africa, where its main focus was Carthage. The community in Rome was the largest in the western part of the empire. The Christianization of the other western provinces lagged far behind that of the eastern empire. Although Christian communities did exist in Gaul, Spain and Britain, they were numerically insignificant.

One reason why Constantine supported Christianity may therefore have been a wish to secure the backing of oriental Christians for his campaign against Licinius, his rival emperor in the east. In the decades before Constantine, Christian communities had undergone repeated bouts of persecution triggered partly by their refusal to accept the juxtaposition, on equal terms, of the empire's multiplicity of religions. The Romans were pragmatically tolerant of the various religions of the peoples they subjugated. Many of these were incorporated in their own pantheon, others continued to exist in their own right. All that was expected was that all Rome's subjects occasionally paid reverence to the Roman gods. The Christians refused to do this. The Romans had previously had the same trouble with the Jews, whose god was exclusive and jealous. 'Thou shalt have no other gods before me' is the first commandment God traditionally imposed upon the Jews on Mount Sinai. Unlike the Christians, however, the Jews were so exclusive that they never strove to convert others. They presented the Romans with a problem, but, until the destruction of Jerusalem in AD 70, only a local one. By contrast, the Christians aspired to impose their god on all the other inhabitants of the Roman Empire. That made them a nuisance. Moreover, Christian missionaries were successful principally with members of the population who felt oppressed and exploited. To slaves or other subject and dependent persons, 'All are equal in the sight of God' was a revolutionary statement, and one the Roman authorities could not tolerate. The empire's traditionalist, conservative thinkers felt that the new cult disturbed the equilibrium between state and religion. But persecution of the Christians never really succeeded in driving the religion beyond the Roman borders; it was too widely entrenched for that. Thus, public policy until Constantine's day alternated between phases of persecution and phases of ignorance.

Constantine began to grant the Christians privileges after his victory over Maxentius in 312, whereas the eastern emperor Licinius continued to back the old gods. Although both emperors had agreed to tolerate all religions equally under the Edict of Milan in 313, neither made any secret of his preference. Constantine's support for Christianity cannot, however, be attributed solely to an attempt to ingratiate himself with Licinius's Christian subjects and turn them against their lord and master. There were simply too few Christians to form a militarily decisive bloc. Edward Gibbon estimates in his *Decline and Fall of the Roman Empire* that in Antioch, Syria's major Christian centre (now Antakiya in Turkey), Christians constituted only a fifth of the population a century after Constantine's death, so how many fewer must there have been in Licinius's time? According to Gibbon, only 50,000 of Rome's one million inhabitants were Christians. This conveys some idea of the difficulties Constantine faced as western emperor when giving the Christians of Rome precedence over the long-established devotees of Jupiter & Co.

Constantine as a monotheist

Thus the key to understanding Constantine's religious policy is probably ideological. In 336, to mark the 30th anniversary of Constantine's reign, Bishop Eusebius, his aforementioned biographer, delivered a speech from which Constantine's motives emerge with considerable clarity. In his address, Eusebius described the harmony between divine and earthly authority. Just as there was only one true God in heaven, so only a lone autocrat could rule the roost on earth. In other words, the absolute monarchy for which Constantine had always striven accorded with the will of God.

Constantine became acquainted with Christianity early on. The tutor of his eldest son Crispus was a professing Christian at a time when the family still resided in Trier and Constantine was only one of four Caesars. From him the future emperor learnt much about that religion. Instead of the many gods of Rome there was only the one god jealous of his exclusivity. One God, one Caesar – Constantine seems to have grasped this equation at an early stage. What fascinated him about Christianity was its monotheism. Rome had many gods and Rome had been a republic for centuries. The Roman emperors, too, had to work with republican institutions. Rome's true traditionalists were republicans who continued to question imperial status two or three centuries after the first emperor, Augustus. The ideological legitimation of the Roman emperors was still fragile. Having a monotheistic religion as a state religion could change that, but in view of Christianity's marginal position within the Roman Empire, Constantine could not simply present himself as a Christian emperor. The whole imperial establishment was heathen. There were probably only a handful of Christian officers in the army, Constantine's real power base, and even they had been soldiers long before they became Christians. Professing Christians did not join the army. In order to emphasize the principle of monotheism, however, Constantine focused on a member of the existing pantheon. Apollo, or his Roman variant, the sun-god Sol, became Constantine's favourite. Sol was honoured on the coins he minted, and he probably visualized the Christian god as a version of that deity.

Support for the Christians was Constantine's ideal way of achieving his monotheism project: one god, one emperor. But it was soon borne in on him that some very practical, earthly difficulties stood in the way of this nice theory. Christian doctrine had yet to become something one could depend on. Different communities subscribed to different views of God, Jesus Christ, and what the latter had allegedly said and done. For a century after it originated, Christian doctrine was based almost entirely on oral traditions handed down to the elders by their predecessors. The letters from the most important missionary, the Apostle Paul, who was never personally acquainted with Jesus, were the first written evidence to be read aloud to congregations. Eventually, when the first devotees began to formulate the story of Jesus in writing, there were not just the four gospels of the New Testament, but some twenty versions of that story, and all of them based on hearsay because none of Jesus's contemporaries had left behind a text on papyrus. Making something of this mess presented a problem which Constantine was quick to tackle. Belief in a single god had to be a uniform belief. The true god who legitimized the true emperor presupposed a single, true, beatifying church. Until Constantine it is hard to speak of a church at all. Communities were in touch with one another, but their supreme authority was their own bishop, who ultimately decided what should be regarded as orthodox within a particular community. Although in contact, Christian communities lived in a decentralized manner.

Constantine strove to change that. Since he also granted material privileges to Christian communities, it could no longer be a matter of indifference to him who within those communities were their rightful recipients. His first challenge was the so-called Donatist controversy in Carthage (now Tunis), the African centre of Christianity. Members

Emperor Constantine. Head of the colossal statue
from the Basilica of Constantine, Rome.

of the community bitterly opposed the choice of a bishop. Some of
them refused to acknowledge him because he had been among those
who had displayed weakness and disavowed their faith when subjected to persecution in earlier years. Constantine tried to support the
bishop by getting some other bishops to pronounce in his favour, but
his opponents ignored this. For the first time, the emperor found he
could do little against perfervid religious zeal, and the North African
Donatists remained in dissent for decades to come.

At the time, however, Constantine had many other concerns that
prompted him to let the matter rest. Not yet the sole ruler he aspired
to be, he still had two rivals in the East who needed removing. This
situation changed after his decisive battle against Licinius in 324,
which took place in the plains west of Byzantium. Now free to con-
centrate on developing the ideological foundation of his emperor-
ship, Constantine took a big step along the road to a state with one
god, one church, and one divinely legitimized emperor.

The Council of Nicaea

In May 325, only a year after his defeat of Licinius outside the gates of Byzantium, Constantine convened the first worldwide ecumenical council of Christian communities. Of the 1,800 bishops invited to attend, some 300 came to Nicaea from all over the empire – even from Persia, where there were a few isolated communities. The meeting at modern Iznik, around 150 kilometres south-east of Istanbul, may be regarded as the birth of the Catholic (in Greek, 'all-embracing') Church. Although not himself an official member of a Christian community, Constantine chaired the assembly in his capacity as a supreme bishop legitimized by God. He acted as moderator and eventually formulated a compromise. The theological occasion for the council was a controversy that would bedevil the Church for centuries – one which Constantine, on his own admission, deemed wholly irrelevant. It concerned the nature of Jesus Christ. Was he 'of the same substance' (Greek: *homoousios*) as God or only 'of like substance' (*homoiousios*)? This question threatened to split the communities just where Christianity was already strong within the empire. Constantine wanted to avoid this at all costs, for what he needed was a single Church, not a whole chorus of dissenting communities with different views.

He provided the bishops with transport, accommodation and other amenities, flattered them and made them feel they were important figures in the great Roman Empire. He was grateful to be of their number, he declared, and he got what he wanted. After weeks of debate, the 300 bishops finally agreed on a formula: Jesus Christ had been begotten by the God the Father and was thus 'of the same substance'. The competing formula 'of like substance' was rejected. This meant that the Church had achieved unity, if only briefly. For the first time in history, Constantine had laid down the following rule of three: one God, one Church, one Emperor.

In 330, five years after the Council of Nicaea, his new imperial residence in Constantinople was inaugurated after extensive building work. Constantine must have found it easy to make Byzantium his capital. He himself had never lived in Rome for long and his ties with the city were few. Several emperors before him had also seldom visited Rome and ruled from Milan or Ravenna, or, like the last sole emperor before Constantine, the great Diocletian, from Nicomedia, modern Izmit, a town midway between Byzantium and Nicaea. The eastern part of the empire had long been its economic powerhouse, and Byzantium was less threatened by the Germans' incessant incursions than the population centres in the west. What clinched Constantine's choice of Byzantium as the new imperial capital, however, was that he could introduce innovations more easily there than if constrained by the historically entrenched structures of Rome. Byzantium was a Greek city that had existed for several centuries before it became part of the Roman Empire in AD 146. When the city was expanded into Constantinople, the new imperial capital, churches as well as prestigious public buildings were erected. Existing pagan shrines were preserved, but their importance perceptibly declined. Constantine also created political institutions that accorded perfectly with his ideas. The new senate was far less influential than the senate of Rome. From the start, Constantinople was the emperor's personal stage.

The Biblical Codex

Almost in passing, this quite alarmingly successful autocrat commissioned another work that has left behind deep and abiding traces. In the interests of Christian unity, Constantine instructed his favourite bishop, Eusebius, to produce 50 books for the capital's many new churches. These compilations of the Christians' recognized sacred texts were to be presented to the various congregations so that the faith would be preached in the same way in every church. The emperor's instruction sounds simpler to carry out than it was in actuality. The Bible as we know it today did not exist. There were individual gospels, stories of the life of Jesus, stories of the Apostles, the letters of Paul and Peter, stories about Jesus's return, and apocalyptic writings that expressed the eschatological expectations of early Christians who believed that the end of the world was nigh. There were also the books of the Jews, some of which had been adopted by the Christians and put together in the Old Testament. Which of these texts should count as doctrinally obligatory for all true 'orthodox Catholic' Christians had yet to be decided in the time of Constantine.[4]

There were practical problems as well. Bishop Eusebius received his commission at a time that represents a watershed in humanity's recording of the written word. Until the 3rd century AD most writing was done on papyrus, which was rolled up for storage purposes. The archives of the ancient world consisted of such scrolls once papyrus had superseded clay tablets, but books already existed in Constantine's day. They consisted of bound sheets, most of them no longer of papyrus but of parchment. Parchment is tanned and specially processed animal hide – either calfskin, sheepskin or goatskin, but in any case, hide taken from domesticated animals whose supply could be controlled.

This parchment, having been rendered as smooth and thin as possible, was written on in special ink by a scribe. Large works necessitated the employment of several scribes at the same time, so regular scribes' workshops came into being. The most famous of these scriptoria were in Alexandria, but Eusebius also had a celebrated scribes' and copyists' workshop in Caesarea at his disposal. Christians had soon begun to record their texts on parchment and bind them into books because these were handier and, in an emergency, more easily hidden than papyrus scrolls. What had not existed until now were complete collections of texts. There were two reasons for this: parchment was very expensive and hard to obtain. Wealthy patrons were required to produce a codex, or book made up of parchment leaves. Moreover, a complete collection of texts was simply too voluminous to be used in times of persecution. The bibles produced by Bishop Eusebius's workshop at Constantine's behest were about 40 centimetres thick and the size of a modern photo album. A whole flock of sheep or several calves would have had to lay down their lives for a single copy. We even know exactly how big the bibles of the time were, because one of the 50 copies so laboriously produced nearly 1,700 years ago has, as if by some miracle, survived to this day.[5]

This is the Codex Sinaiticus, one of the oldest bound books in the world and the oldest example of the New Testament bar none. It survived in the extremely dry climate of the Sinai Desert, hidden and forgotten in the monastery there.

Emperor Constantine, who commissioned the work, is one of the few Roman emperors to die in bed at the zenith of his power. He had just set off from Constantinople on a long-planned campaign against the Persians when he was suddenly taken ill and had to turn back. He died in Nicomedia in May 337, having had himself officially baptized. He left his formal adoption of Christianity until the last moment, in part so as not to offend his non-Christian subjects, but mainly because he wanted to enter the Christian paradise free from sin. He had been assured that baptism would wash away all his sins, so anyone baptized on the threshold of death entered the presence of God unblemished. Constantine was a very calculating Christian, therefore, but history has thoroughly confirmed the wisdom of his strategy.

Christianity provided the East Roman Empire with an ideological foundation that would prove extremely robust. As an institution for the wielding of power, the God-anointed emperor was unbeatable. For all the dynastic upheavals and personal failings of Constantine's successors, people clung to their emperor by the grace of God. The East Roman Byzantine Empire survived for an incredibly long time: no less than 1,123 years.[6]

The Obsessive

Constantin Tischendorf in search of the
original text of the New Testament

Cairo, 12 April 1844

I found myself obliged to leave Alexandria far earlier than I had at first wished. It was upon the morning of Easter Sunday that I embarked on board a vessel to proceed up the Nile to the ancient capital of the Caliphs. On the preceding evening, for the first time this year, the fearsome khamsin had begun to blow; what I had mistaken for the sunset's rosy glow was nothing other than bright red sandy dust swept up from the desert and permeating the atmosphere. Even after six p.m. the heat had remained excessive; during the night the howling storm had disturbed my slumbers, but this morning it seemed to me as if even the sun of Egypt were celebrating Holy Easter. The cheerful aspect of the morning surprised us all, and a wind was blowing which made the navigation of the Nile practicable. This was quite a new adventure for me; but as I was travelling with the physician returning from Paris to Cairo, it was rendered easy enough. [...] In our vessel we had, besides, seven Arabs as sailors. Upon our embarking, they were at their meal: seated in a circle, they scooped up their pilaf with their fingers, which appeared very clean, out of a big family dish common to all; and this during our whole excursion was their main form of sustenance. [...] On our leaving them they were pleased to be presented with a goodly piece of mutton, nor did they spurn a glass of our wine. [...]

I had not reflected upon the possible dangers of our Nile voyage until, close to the junction of the canal with the river, we met a vessel that had been blown upon her beam-ends by the wind. This vessel was but a trifle smaller than ours. Six men, all good swimmers, were carrying ashore a female passenger who had drowned. The result of this melancholy

Constantin Tischendorf in Paris, c. 1841.

spectacle was that, without hesitation, we permitted our sailors to take refuge in a cove whenever they deemed the current too fierce or the place at all dangerous.

The banks of the Nile are not to be compared with those of the Seine or the Rhine, but they have their own peculiar beauty, and my eye revelled in many a new delight. [...] The colour of the water of the Nile was the pale, muddy yellow of the Tiber at Rome. I was eager to taste it, for who can fail to know how famed it is for its excellence! My friend the physician told me it was most wholesome without filtering. [...] And in fact, notwithstanding its suspect appearance, it tasted far from unpleasant. [...]

At noon on the fourth day we saw the tips of the pyramids. I took them at first to be the tops of the masts and sails of craft not far ahead of us – but it was really the pyramids! [...] As evening approached, and as we yet saw nothing of Shubra [the suburb where Mehmet Ali, viceroy of Egypt, lived, J.G.], *we gave up hope of reaching Cairo before nightfall. Suddenly, however, a favourable breeze sprang up, but so strong that it wanted but a couple of inches to plunge one side of our vessel in the water; we flew rapidly past Shubra, which was brilliantly illuminated. Between eight and nine, after being carried some forty paces through shallow water upon the shoulders of our Arabs, we landed safely at Bulak. It is true that we arrived in Cairo at an unpropitious moment, for we found the gate already closed and were ignorant of the password; but my companion knew how to solve the problem. He called through the gate to the guard that he came in his capacity as Hakim Bashi (senior physician) direct from Mehmet Ali at Shubra, whither he had been suddenly summoned. As soon as the credulous guard had opened the gate, even in default of any identification (every physician wears a government badge), we entered without more ado.*[1]

Constantin Tischendorf reached Cairo aboard his Nile dhow in April 1844. The Leipzig theologian who here gives such a measured account of his adventures in the East was at that time just twenty-nine years old, but he was already an experienced traveller. He had already been on the move for four years when he boarded a steamer at Leghorn bound for Alexandria. He had visited several European capitals, had spent two years in Paris, and had even obtained a private audience with the Pope. Why should the Nile and Cairo have overawed him? Having begun by checking into the Grand Hôtel de l'Orient, a luxury establishment, he had to change location after a few days and moved for financial reasons into the Casa Pini, *in a genuine Cairo street where even meeting a rider on donkeyback can be awkward.* He could now view the city only from the roof of the hotel, but he made the most of this, particularly at sunset, when he never neglected *to stroll for pleasure* there. He thoroughly relished what he saw, including the *countless minarets and scattered palm trees that rear their heads above the houses huddled there. I also behold small gardens, planted with stately trees, laid out upon some of the neighbouring roofs.* Tischendorf soon perceived that much of family life in Cairo took place on its flat roofs, and he set down his own reflections on this: *As many of the houses are, in a certain sense, open at the top, the muezzins or summoners to prayer could doubtless look down from the minarets of the mosques upon many an agreeable family scene, were not almost all of them blind. But their very blindness may be a recommendation for their post; for the Egyptian is extremely jealous of any participation in his domestic recreations, and especially of even the most innocent glimpse of his wives.*[2]

Tischendorf was an attentive and interested observer of his surroundings. Cairo fascinated him above all as a melting pot for the most varied races and religions. *There are Arabs in their dreamy repose; Turks in thoughtless self-sufficiency; Persians with pride in their eyes and splendour in their attire; Armenians with manly, handsome features and dark beards; Copts with brownish-yellow faces full of dark mistrust; Greek monks in their black robes, cunning falsehood in their treacherous gaze; Bedouins most picturesque in their* keffiyeh, *with a hempen rope about their brow, the freedom of the desert in all their movements; handsome negro boys who are happy enough in the red* tarboosh *and the gay attire with which their masters bedeck them; peasant women with a dirty shift over their voluminous trousers, large rings in their ears, often, too in their noses, and many gold coins around their necks. […] Suddenly, an Englishman pushes through the throng with his lady on a donkey. A French physician, his sabre at his side, comes riding along on a magnificent grey, his footman making way for him.*

On one side a harem is proceeding to the bathhouse, enveloped from head to foot in black silk cloaks; the face, excepting the eyes, concealed by white drapery. These women, riding upon handsomely caparisoned donkeys, move silent and ghostlike through the throng. The baths themselves are almost as sumptuous in appearance as the mosques.

I cannot forbear to pause outside a barbershop. It drives every other thought from one's mind to watch a head being lathered, then shaved to a lunar disk with a razor – bare save for the Mohammedan lock of hair fluttering in its midst. [...]

The dust at this season of the year would be a most oppressive nuisance, were not more than a thousand donkeys constantly traversing the city and sprinkling it with water-hoses, a regulation which does great credit to the sanitary police, for it is of the utmost importance to the poor ophthalmic sufferers who abound here in melancholy profusion. The number of the totally blind in Cairo itself is greater than is to be found in the entire population of many other countries. One of the privileges of these blind persons pleased me: they alone are permitted to be on the street after nightfall without a lantern. The nooks and crannies of the streets and the public gardens are all too often their only home. How many times, when returning at a late hour, have I not stumbled over the bodies of the poor blind natives lying about! At Cairo great attention is paid to the education of the blind, and the office of muezzin is not the only one open to them.[3]

But fascinated as he allowed himself to be by daily life in Cairo, Constantin Tischendorf had not come to the Orient to get to know the people there. He had a mission, and Cairo was only its starting point. Despite his youth, Tischendorf was a specialist and one of the internationally acknowledged experts in his field. He was a palaeographer, a decipherer of ancient manuscripts.

He discovered his enthusiasm for ancient texts at an early age. At his secondary school in Plauen, Saxony, he was one of the outstanding pupils at Greek and Latin. Born on 18 January 1815 at Lengenfeld in Saxonian Vogtland, he came from a family of academics – his father was Lengenfeld's forensic physician – in which it went without saying that the boys would also graduate from university. Constantin was the ninth of eleven children, but six of his siblings died soon after birth, so he grew up with one sister and three brothers. He remained in close, lifelong touch with his older brother Julius. His granddaughter Hildegard Behrend reports that he was also very close to his mother. It was with her, according Behrend, that he planned his career after leaving school and going on to Leipzig University at Easter 1834.

Tischendorf enrolled in courses in theology and philosophy. He also attended lectures on literature but soon abandoned them. Instead, he himself wrote some rapturously romantic poems of which he published a slender volume in 1838 under the title *Maiknospen* [Buds of May]. He further demonstrated his penchant for the rapturous – or, in theological terms, the mystical – in a novella he published in 1839 under the pseudonym Dr Fritz. *Der junge Mystiker oder die drei letzten Festzeiten aus seinem Leben* [The Young Mystic or the Three Last Feast Days of His Life] was an autobiographically-coloured book about a very personal quest for God.

In this work, Constantin Tischendorf took up his position in the theological debate then in progress at Germany's major universities. It concerned the irruption of Enlightenment into theology. Critical minds had begun to question the historical content and plausibility of the Bible. Although it had several forerunners, *Das Leben Jesu* [The Life of Jesus] by David Friedrich Strauss, published in 1835, a year after Tischendorf arrived at university, became a milestone in historico-critical research into the Bible. To his supporters, Strauss was the man who finally disposed of the belief in miracles and put the mythical interpretation of the Bible in its proper place. For a start, he stated that even if only a generation separated the death of Jesus from the writing of the gospels, 'that time in itself is sufficient to pervade the historical with the mythical'. In his book on historical research into the life of Jesus, published in 1906, the celebrated theologian and medical missionary Albert Schweitzer describes what an immense impression Strauss left behind. His predecessors, said Schweitzer, 'had apprehensively wondered what is left of the historical Jesus if one ventures to apply the concept of the myth consistently. Strauss does not have this problem. Hegel's philosophy liberated him. Hegel's conception of idea and reality enlightened him.'[4]

The crux of Strauss's criticism of the transfiguration of Jesus and his miracles as recounted in the various gospels, is that most of them had no connection with contemporary reality. In his view, the stories in the New Testament harked back to religious myths in the Old Testament. 'It is, therefore, almost *a priori* irrefutable to assume that the historical Jesus will present himself to us clothed in Old Testament, messianic ideas and early Christian expectations.'

But for all his criticism of the mythical superimpositions upon the historical Jesus, Strauss clung to the central idea of religion: 'This idea of God-humanity as the goal of humankind to be realized in every personality is the eternally real element in the person of Jesus that no criticism can destroy.'

Being a romantic and an adherent of conservative theology, Constantin Tischendorf was far from content with this view of Jesus. To him the Bible was God's sacred revelation, word for word, and not to be called into question. We have few direct allusions to the controversy dating from his student days. However, looking back on them in an obituary dedicated to his principal academic mentor, Professor Johann Georg Benedikt Winer, he mentioned that Winer's maxim 'Protestantism is, by its very nature, related to science' had absolutely nothing to do with *rationalistic superficiality and conceptual dilution or the Hegelian evaporation of revealed truths.*

In this respect, Tischendorf was so much at one with his doctoral supervisor that he wasted few words on the subject. Not so his epigones, who dressed the whole thing up in very dramatic garb. His son-in-law Ludwig Schneller describes the situation as follows in his Tischendorf memoir: 'That was the time when famous German theologians, in the belief that they were serving the cause of historical truth, did their utmost and employed the most drastic methods of scientific research to prove the inauthenticity of most New Testament texts, and thus, as it were, to blow out the light of the New Testament.' Even a century later, Ludwig Schneller, himself a cleric brought up in a missionary's household in Palestine, was utterly outraged by these shameless attacks on God's word. 'They conceded the authenticity of only four of Paul the Apostle's epistles and pronounced all the rest poor stuff of later years. Those learned gentlemen totally rejected the four Gospels in particular, and St John's Gospel found least favour in their sight. There were doubtless powerful witnesses at German universities who firmly opposed these earthshaking allegations, but by others, who purported to be the sole owners of science, they were derided as unscientific and old-fashioned.' In view of this situation, said Schneller, Tischendorf resolved to take up the cudgels and 'drive the foe from the field with the weapons of science'.[5] Tischendorf could, however, proceed upon the assumption that this battle would present little risk to himself. Contrary to the assertions of Schneller and others, it was not people like David Friedrich Strauss who called the tune at universities. On the contrary, Strauss's book cost him his academic career. Pietists and other conservative ecclesiastical circles saw to it that he lost his post at Tübingen and could not take up a chair at Zurich later on. Strauss came under such strong pressure that he had begun to recant when an inheritance rendered him so financially independent that he was able to dispense with a university appointment altogether.

Tischendorf's attitude, by contrast, was not risky at all, save possibly to the extent that it made him bite off more than he could chew. He was what we would now call an evangelical, but like his mentor Johann Georg Benedikt Winer he regarded himself as a Protestant scientist through and through. It was his hubris to believe that he could prove the truth of the Bible scientifically. Winer, whose principal work was a grammar of the New Testament, had taught him scientific textual criticism, so he had to concede, reluctantly, that many critics were correct in pointing out discrepancies in different editions of the Bible. The poor situation as regards sources presented critics of the historical Jesus with plenty of scope for attacks. Tischendorf's training, together with his inclinations and abilities, motivated him to grapple with precisely this problem. Once on the trail, he started work on a critical edition of the Greek New Testament, all the original early texts being written in Greek.

However, because both his parents unexpectedly died within a year of each other (his father in 1835, his mother in 1836), Tischendorf had first to earn a living. He hastened to gain his doctorate of philosophy in 1838, then went to live in the home of the Reverend Ferdinand Leberecht Zehme in Grossstädeln, now Markkleeberg, near Leipzig, where he became a private tutor. He no doubt felt that his 18 months there were intellectually undemanding, because he embarked on preparations for his Greek edition of the New Testament in addition to his tutorial activities. Nevertheless, Grossstädeln proved to be a watershed in his life because it was there that he met and fell in love with Angelika Zehme, the parson's daughter. Constantin and Angelika, then 23 and 16 respectively, kept their feelings to themselves for the time being. After Tischendorf had returned to Leipzig to qualify as a lecturer they exchanged love letters in which he also, however, made it clear that he had a special vocation, a divine mission that would not allow him to waste his genius. Granddaughter Hildegard Behrend quotes a letter he wrote Angelika in July 1840, a few months before he left Saxony for several years:

But question the innermost reasons for your love, my dear Angelika! Do you love the earnestness with which this young man gazes into the future; the conscientiousness with which he makes the most of his talents; the devout strength with which he contends against his mind's ungodly passions; the firmness and resolve with which he holds to what he acknowledges to be holy and true; the love with which he cleaves to dear hearts without guile or perfidy? Then you have a right and a guarantee for yourself if you love me in the way you say and write that you do. And my own guarantee shall be my admission that I love in you what will endure beyond the fleeting moment of youth, what I esteem to be the bloom of sacred virginity in the hope that life will bear delightful fruit in time to come.[6]

In this letter, Tischendorf was preparing Angelika for the fact that no official engagement, still less marriage, was imminent, and that he must first make the most of his 'special talents', in other words, his gift for ancient texts and languages. He had no intention of ending his days as a teacher or settling down as a parish priest. Together with his professor, Benedikt Winer, he had long ago set his sights on an academic career. In October 1840 he habilitated, or qualified as a lecturer, with the foreword to his new edition of the Greek New Testament. Others now spend years on their habilitation, whereas he virtually completed this formality with the foreword to the work that really interested him. What did the Greek New Testament look like in its original form? Such was the question that exercised him throughout his life. Tischendorf combined several things: his belief in the Bible's divine revelation, which he wanted to buttress scientifically; his great gifts; and his ambition as a researcher. Above all, though, he hoped to go down in history as the man famed for reconstructing the original version of the New Testament out of all available sources. He became positively obsessed with this aim, in fact he more than once describes himself as driven, as a person predestined by God. He was armed with an enormous ego that enabled him, without hesitation, to tackle tasks that others had abandoned as soon as they grasped the problems they entailed.

While working on his edition of the Greek New Testament, he had already travelled to southern Germany, Switzerland and Strasbourg to look for ancient Greek manuscripts in libraries there. He began to make a careful study of which libraries harboured which treasures where, and he wanted to examine, compare and check all available manuscripts with a view to 'harvesting' them for his new original text.

Europe then possessed three 4th- or 5th-century biblical manuscripts that provided the oldest extant documentary evidence of early Christianity. The so-called Codex Alexandrinus, a 5th-century Greek manuscript containing large parts of the Old Testament and some sections of the New, was in the possession of the British Museum and is now in the British Library. Demonstrably in the library of the Alexandrian patriarchate from the 11th century onwards, this biblical manuscript from Alexandria in Egypt was in 1627 presented by Patriarch Kyrillos Loukaris to King Charles I of England. The British Museum had produced a scientifically-competent treatment and translation of it even in Tischendorf's day, so there were no more laurels for the young German scholar to win in London.

The second and most important manuscript was in the care of the Vatican. Dating from the 4th century, it was at that time the oldest known biblical text, containing large parts of the Old Testament and some fragments of the New. To Tischendorf, this treasure was an unattainable object of desire throughout his life. Not only did the Vatican guard its manuscript jealously, but, at the same time that Tischendorf was setting out to conquer the world of the Ur-Bible, it was itself engaged in preparing an edition in readable Greek. Being still a nobody in the field of scholarship, Tischendorf concluded that he had no chance of personally examining the Codex Vaticanus.

That left the Codex Ephraemi. To initiates this codex was a famous or infamous palimpsest on which several experts had already broken their teeth. A palimpsest is an overwritten parchment. In this instance, an ancient biblical manuscript from the 5th century had been overwritten in the 12th with treatises by Ephraim the Syrian, a Doctor of the Church. Parchment being very expensive, scribes often used it more than once by scraping off the original text and writing over it. The impression of the original text generally remained legible, but in the Codex Ephraemi's case the original text was so thoroughly effaced that, despite repeated attempts, no one had succeeded in deciphering more than a few sentences. The manuscript was preserved in the French National Library in Paris, and it was generally assumed that the original text had been lost forever.

This was where Constantin Tischendorf saw his chance. While still engaged on his habilitation he prepared to undertake an expedition to the Seine. He applied to Saxony's Minister of Education for a bursary to enable him to research the Codex Ephraemi. Because he was promised only a small sum from that source, he borrowed money from his family. Julius Tischendorf, who had followed in their father's footsteps and had already obtained a public medical examiner's post in Lengenfeld, was willing to give his younger brother a helping hand. This was still not enough, but Tischendorf felt so convinced that the Parisian codex was only waiting for him to crack it that he staked everything on a single card: he took out a life insurance policy and immediately raised money on it. Altogether, he now had enough to live on very frugally for some time.

On 30 October 1840, when Tischendorf boarded a stagecoach and set off for Paris, he had no idea that he was turning his back on his home and Angelika for several years. At the National Library in Paris, the 25-year-old from Leipzig was greeted with surprise and incredulity when he announced that he had come to decipher the Codex Ephraemi, which so many people had already tried without success. The first was the Swiss theologian Johann Jakob Wettstein in the 18th century. He failed to decipher more than a very few fragmentary sentences, although they did prove that the manuscript was a Greek uncial of the Bible (that is, unpunctuated and written in capitals) probably dating from the 5th century. Then came Johann Jakob Griesbach, a German professor who had made a name for himself in biblical research by producing the first synoptic edition of the New Testament. After visiting Paris, Griesbach reported that the librarians had assured him that no mortal man could read the script, which was positively evanescent. He tried and soon gave up. Six years before Tischendorf arrived on the scene, the French had made another attempt to render the hidden text legible with the aid of some newly developed chemicals. The Leipzig theologian Hase, who was in Paris at the time and had watched the experiment, gave the following description of what happened: 'The result was so unsatisfactory that, even with the resources of the French government, editing the text is impracticable in view of the manuscript's condition.'

The librarians thought Tischendorf was suffering from delusions of grandeur, and no wonder, but they let him have his way. With iron discipline, the ambitious young German wrestled with the codex day after day for two long years. He later described his work as follows:

The restoration of the script [after chemical treatment, J.G.] *is very uneven. One sheet looks more brown and blackish, another more green and blue. The later script, written in dark black, has run into the earlier in varying degrees. But the rescriptor's procedure has rendered the already fine parchment so thin at many points that the letters on the reverse show through and lead to errors; the parchment is also pierced and torn in many places. Thus, in spite of its chemical refreshment, deciphering the script has remained so difficult that, for all my preliminary studies, I have become familiar with the fragments only after laboriously reading them three times over; that I have often espied the outline of hidden letters thanks only to an opportune ray of sunshine; and that, under these circumstances, the codex could have lain in Paris for another century, i.e. until it fell asleep forever, before a French eye caressed it like mine.*[7]

To the Parisian librarians' mounting surprise, Tischendorf spent two years ploughing his way through a total of 290 folio sheets of New Testament fragments. Thanks to an immensely self-assured knowledge of the text, great familiarity with ancient Greek uncial script, a good eye, and incredible perseverance, he succeeded in deciphering page after page of the hidden script until *all that remains unread amounts to no more than one page.*[8]

This achievement instantly catapulted him into the world's small circle of leading palaeographers and brought him plenty of recognition. He received an honorary doctorate from a Prussian university, three 'non-German governments' including the Vatican invested him with orders, and the Dutch struck a new medal for outstanding scientific achievement especially in his honour. Published by Tauchnitz of Leipzig in 1843, the Codex Ephraemi was, so to speak, Tischendorf's apprentice piece. The door to his future career had now opened. He was under the protection of the court of Saxony. Apart from King Friedrich August II, it was primarily Prince Johann of Saxony, himself interested in Tischendorf's type of biblical research, who backed the rising star in the scholarly heavens. But Tischendorf gained some private sponsors for his work in addition to the court of Saxony. The fact that he also became a regular contributor to the *Augsburger Allgemeine,* the leading newspaper for the educated German middle class during the 19th century, not only enabled him to publicize his own successes but naturally earned him fees for his articles.

Although only 27 years old, Constantin Tischendorf was now a somebody. Otherwise than two years earlier, he hoped it would now be possible for him to gain access to the Codex Vaticanus. He requested and received a letter of recommendation from Prince Johann of Saxony to Pope Gregory XVI. He was further endorsed by the then Archbishop of Paris, Denis-Auguste Affre, on whom his work on the Codex Ephraemi had clearly left a lasting impression, and also, of course, by the Saxon chargé d'affaires at the Vatican and various other influential persons with access to the Vatican hierarchy. Tischendorf arrived in Rome at the end of February 1843 and spent four months there in a vain endeavour to get at the Codex Vaticanus. Although no one he spoke with actually said no, he was effectively blocked behind the scenes. At the same time, Cardinal Mai, who had been toiling away at an edition of the Codex for twelve years – the work was largely complete except for the introductory prolegomenon – assured him of his personal esteem. Mai complained of his fragile health, which represented the reason for the delay in publication. He showed Tischendorf five completed volumes, four of them relating to the Old Testament and one to the New, and left him the New Testament volume to read. Tischendorf read it and was horrified. What he found was not a transcription of the ancient uncial script into readable Greek, in other words, not a treatment faithful to the original text. He had, he wrote later, *been given some printed example amended to accord with the Vatican version: a procedure that may have resulted in numerous infractions.*[9]

This only intensified Tischendorf's eagerness to gain access to the original. Even as he chatted with well-disposed cardinals, however, the decision had long ago gone against him behind the walls of the Vatican. The second most powerful man in Vatican City, Cardinal Lambruschini, informed Platner, the Saxon chargé d'affaires, that his request had been denied 'because His Holiness does not wish it'. Tischendorf, who refused to believe this, pressed for a personal audience with the Pope. Several weeks later he was actually granted an audience subject to a proviso: that the subject of the Codex Vaticanus might not be raised. The account Tischendorf later wrote of his meeting with Gregory XVI for the *Augsburger Allgemeine* is indicative of the up-and-coming scholar's self-image. According to Tischendorf, he shone and the Pope marvelled at his brilliance. Tischendorf spoke Latin but the Pope quickly switched to Italian, evidently because his Latin wasn't too fluent. They talked about Tischendorf's work hitherto, for which the Pope was apparently full of praise. Eventually, Tischendorf did after all complain about the proviso governing the audience and said that Cardinal Lambruschini had refused to let him see the Codex Vaticanus. And lo, it seems that *the shrewd old man* knew nothing of this affront to the young German and promised to make enquiries. Tischendorf, who thereafter believed that he would be able to attain his goal, waited impatiently for the manuscript to be submitted to him. The rejection was, in fact, modified and he was allowed a sight of the Codex Vaticanus. But what a disappointment: instead of being permitted to work on the text and undertake its decipherment and transcription, he was given only three hours on two successive days to examine the precious relic. He was allowed to taste, but not to eat.

This setback in Rome helped to mature a decision that Tischendorf had been incubating for a considerable time. What, he had asked himself while working in Paris, if he himself endeavoured to supplement the only three known examples of Greek biblical manuscripts from the early days of Christianity with a discovery of his own? *Our European libraries derived the treasures I pursued largely from the monasteries of the Orient, in which, from early centuries onward, sacred and other writings were copied by diligent monks and collected from all quarters. Was it not possible that one or another literary monument still lay hidden in some corner of these Greek, Coptic, Armenian and Syrian monasteries? Would not any sheet of parchment bearing written evidence from the fifth, sixth or seventh century be a little treasure, a substantial enrichment of Christian knowledge?*[10]

In the winter of 1842, when his work in Paris had only just ended, Tischendorf began sounding out the court of Saxony and his other patrons, who were now numerous, to see if he could count on financial support for an expedition to the Orient. He titillated his princely protector in Dresden with thoughts of the prestige that would accrue were a Saxon – not an Englishman or a Frenchman, whose nations had hitherto shared out the bulk of the salvaged treasures of antiquity between them – to score a bull's-eye in the search for ancient biblical texts. And indeed, Tischendorf managed to persuade the royal house to finance his expedition. From Venice on 14 November 1843 he wrote as follows to Angelika, his secret fiancée: *The Ministry of Culture has placed me in an excellent position to head for the Orient. I received this news with tears of delight. I feel as if I am going to a great, sacred Christmas of which our own, with its candlelit trees and gifts, are only pale reflections. How blessed I am by God!*[11]

It totally escaped him that his beloved back home in Grossstädeln, who had now been waiting for her Constantin for almost three years, might not be quite as delighted by the fact that, instead of returning, he now proposed to set out on a really long journey. *Destiny is wresting me away by force; I must obey.*

However, it was another few months before Tischendorf could embark on his great adventure in the East. He had various arrangements to make and wanted to visit the last interesting libraries in Italy he had yet to see. Moreover, sea travel across the Mediterranean in the depths of winter was no pleasure, so it was not until March that he finally sailed from Leghorn aboard a ship that conveyed him to Alexandria by way of Sicily, Malta and Greece. Before leaving he had told his brother Julius in a high-flown letter how much he hankered after the Orient. *I wish to see Jerusalem, regardless of the voices of happiness and pleasure and love that can lure one away from one's goal.* He countered the remonstrances of his brother, who had urged him to return to Leipzig, with no less an argument than the *Iliad*, and quoted Priam's response when his wife Hecuba tries to dissuade him from going to the Greek camp to fetch slain Hector's corpse: *Do not hold me back that have resolved to go, nor yourself be a bird of ill omen in my house; you speak in vain.* Typically enough, Constantin Tischendorf advised his brother to read the verses in Greek, because only then did they really achieve their full effect. Even in the event of his not surviving the journey, he consoled himself as follows: *Were I never to return home, I know I would have perished doing my best. The warrior must remain on the battlefield, and you know my battlefield. I would then, on my way to the earthly Jerusalem, have found the celestial one. Blossoming earth is lovely; sacred heaven must be lovelier still.*[12]

But the voyage promptly subjected his courage to a drastic test. The passage to Malta was a stormy one. Off Greece they were beset by a storm so violent that Tischendorf clung to his bunk in despair, and even when the ship reached Alexandria it could not put in: *The approach to the harbour of Alexandria being too dangerous to be navigated in the darkness of night, our vessel tacked to and fro off the entrance for several hours; and, as often as it turned, it produced the most unpleasant motion. How I rejoiced when we dropped anchor in the morning!*[13]

View of the bell tower in St Catherine's Monastery.

The Last Byzantines

The desert monks live much as they did 1,500 years ago

It was still pitch-dark when my alarm clock went off at 5.00 a.m. I had been unable to make out much of the monastery the night before, and it was just as hard to get my bearings now. It must have been a few years since the monastery was in total darkness at night, as the place was dimly illuminated by a light or two. It wasn't hard to make out the church, but harder to find my way to the entrance via alleyways and winding flights of steps. I had really been expecting that around 6.00 a.m., when early Mass was officially due to start, some monks would file into the church and I would be able to unobtrusively join them, but I was wide of the mark. Shortly before six I was the only person around. The church, too, seemed totally deserted. No light could be seen, neither through the panes of coloured glass in the outer door through which one entered the narthex, the antechamber to the nave itself, nor in the church's upper windows. Six o'clock Mass was something of an exaggeration, I told myself, so I was rather surprised to find that the door, instead of being locked, opened easily.

I had been inside Greek Orthodox churches a few times in Istanbul, but only on festive occasions like Christmas or Easter, so what I now saw was unfamiliar to me. The church seemed entirely deserted save for two monks standing at a pair of lecterns a few metres in front of the iconostasis. Each of these lecterns, which stood facing one another at the end of the nave at a distance of some five metres, had a spotlight hanging immediately above its rotatable top. The spotlights, which illuminated nothing but the books on the lecterns, were the only electric lights in the church. The rest of the lighting was provided by candles in big chandeliers or small coloured lamps suspended from the lofty ceiling, substantially obscuring one's view of the iconostasis and the chancel beyond. Only the two monks at their lecterns were clearly visible. They were intoning a liturgical song, turn and turn about. The melody meandered along, relatively unmodulated and interrupted only by the periodic Kyrie eleison (Lord, have mercy) that marked a boundary between song and prayer.

As I discovered in due course, this chanting resembles a carpet of sound that underlies the whole Mass. Everything seems rather trancelike, and the diffuse candlelight reinforces one's sense of unreality. The liturgy adheres to the Byzantine rite and has remained more or less unchanged for 1,500 years. The Sinaite monks are Basilians; they observe the rule of St Basil, who lived from 329 to 379. Their chanting is done in ancient Greek (Koine) and is probably incomprehensible to most of those attending Mass. Koine is the name of the Greek lingua franca that evolved from various Greek dialects in the course of Alexander's campaigns circa 300 BC and became the predominant language in the eastern Mediterranean. The New Testament was written in Koine, as was the so-called Septuagint, a translation of the Old Testament into Greek. After West and East Rome separated, Koine became the official language of the Byzantine Empire. Even if one critically questions and tries to avoid the arrogantly Western view of the Eastern Church which Tischendorf adopted towards the monks, this form of divine service seems almost as exotic to someone socialized in Protestant Christendom as a lamaist ritual in a Tibetan monastery.

Also involved in addition to the two monks with their constant, alternate chanting are one or two priests who initially remain in the chancel behind the iconostasis. The ceremony is borrowed from ancient Greek theatre. At precisely determined junctures the priests emerge from the chancel through the open door in the iconostasis. There are different appearances or 'entrances' that serve different liturgical purposes. In the Little Entrance the priest either swings a censer or carries a gospel or an icon in front of him. With this he circles the church once, and individual members of the congregation can step forward and kiss the icon. The Great Entrance is the prelude to Communion. The priest enters the space in front of the iconostasis with the sacraments, the wine and consecrated bread, in his hands. Otherwise than in the Catholic Church, the Eucharist or Communion is celebrated by all members of the congregation. Anyone who wishes gets the consecrated bread and a mouthful of wine from a spoon. Special unconsecrated bread known as antidoron is distributed to those who do not wish to participate in the Eucharist.

Unlike the Orthodox churches I attended in Istanbul, the Sinaite monastic community has no sermons or communal singing. Towards the end of Mass, after the priest has blessed them, members of the congregation line up to receive the antidoron. The service lasts around two hours, and there is something very contemplative about its monotony. Although attendance at church signifies a communal service to God, everyone is there for themselves. The service is a meditative submersion; addresses to the congregation or biblical exegeses play no role. Only one monk takes no part in the meditation, being almost continuously engaged in lighting certain candles and extinguishing others. For the latter purpose he uses a blowpipe operated not with his mouth but with a bulb the size of a tennis ball.

It was some time before my eyes became accustomed to the gloom and I gradually made out more people in the church. Greek Orthodox churches have no pews, just some tall chairs standing against the walls or, as at St Catherine's, flanking the nave and marking it off from the two side aisles. The chairs in the monastery church are accessible from both the nave and the aisles. For this reason, it was a while before I noticed some churchgoers and monks standing in the aisles. Most of the monks and the pilgrims visiting the monastery fold up the seats and stand there with only their arms resting on the backs, it being thought presumptuous in the Orthodox Church to serve God sitting down. As time went by the church was also filled with pilgrims who had spent the night elsewhere. Although one cannot sit down, nobody minds if people walk in or out while the service is in progress. It is also customary to move around during a service. Not only do many worshippers fall to their knees or even prostrate themselves, but they also stroll into the narthex to light candles or walk past the gallery of icons in the side aisles, praying. Thus, every member of the congregation structures his or her own programme while the hours-long Mass is in progress.[1]

When the sun rose outside and its rays reached the church's upper windows, the nocturnal Mass lost its magic and the church, monastery and monks gradually took shape.

The church in St Catherine's Monastery

Before gaining my first sight of the whole monastery by daylight, I took a closer look at the church now that it was light outside. The central nave, with its lofty ceiling and two side aisles separated from it by columns, is such as one would find in many Roman Catholic churches. The difference that strikes one at once is the iconostasis that conceals the chancel and the semicircular apse. There are no pews either, the nave being an open, carpeted space whose front half is used by priests and monks, the rear half by churchgoers and pilgrims. The Orthodox Church treats the nave of a basilica as a continuation of the area in which liturgical services take place. The church's ante-chamber, or narthex, separated from the main body of the church by a tall and very imposing double door, extends across the full width of the building. In the Sinai church the side aisles are accessible from the narthex by way of two smaller doors. It is probable that pilgrims used not to be allowed to enter the church through the imposing central door. Several metres high and at least four metres wide, this main portal is of cedarwood, richly adorned with carving, and dates from the 6th century, when the church was built. It is the oldest known wooden door in any church anywhere. The Sinai church was built in 560 by order of Emperor Justinian of Byzantium, Constantine's best-known successor, who also built Hagia Sophia in Constantinople. Together with its defensive wall, which was also built under Justin-ian, the monastery has preserved its original form to the present day.[2]

The mosaics in the apse, which is largely hidden from the ordi-nary churchgoer by the iconostasis and a crucified Christ that reaches almost to the ceiling, constitute the Sinai church's special treasure. It is only when walking through the iconostasis from one of the side aisles that one sees the mosaic in the dome of the apse above the covered altar. Hovering in the centre is Christ Pantocrator, flanked by Elias and Moses and with the Apostles John, Peter and James at his feet. Like the cedarwood door, the mosaic dates from the 6th century and is an exquisite artefact from the heyday of the Byzantine Empire. But the church's real highlight is to be found behind the nave. Built around the end of the church are three chapels of which the lateral ones are original and the central one was inserted later. Where the

19th-century view of the nave in the basilica.

latter now stands there used to be a courtyard accessible from the two side chapels. All this little courtyard contained was a green bush, but that thorn bush was the biblical reason for building the entire monastery. It was said to be the burning bush from which God commanded Moses to remove his shoes and receive his orders. Today, the spot where the thorn bush used to be is covered by a marble slab with a small altar above it. The whole chapel is adorned with faiences and carpeted, a form of decoration very reminiscent of a mosque. Also like a mosque, the monastery's holy of holies may not be entered with one's shoes on.

The church is not very big, all in all, and would not hold many more than 200 people. With its chandeliers, candelabra and lights suspended from the ceiling, its carpeted flagstones and ubiquitous icons, it makes a warm, almost homely impression. And indeed, the monks spend a large proportion of their time in this architectural and spiritual centre of the entire complex. Although the denizens of the monastery disperse and pursue their various occupations when not at Mass, they congregate here several times a day and during the night. The Orthodox Church attaches more importance to display than the Catholic and far more than the Protestant, hence the gilded iconostases that cut off the holy of holies, the chancel, from ordinary members of the congregation. Hence, too, the priests' gorgeous vestments, which they often, like stage actors, change more than once in the course of Mass. The Bibles or so-called Evangeliaries are bound in silver or gold, the church walls adorned with mosaics and frescos. Believers are meant to be impressed by this splendour in accordance with the maxim: 'Only the best is good enough for God.' Although the relatively small basilica in the Sinai monastery does not cultivate the same splendour as a large cathedral, it is a treasure house nonetheless.[3]

Art historians make pilgrimages to Sinai solely to admire the monastery's collection of icons, which is almost unrivalled. The uniqueness of the collection of icons in St Catherine's Monastery stems from the fact that it contains examples from the 6th century to the present day. This is because Sinai did not observe the ban on images imposed in Byzantium between 726 and 843. While icons were being destroyed in Constantinople, they continued to be painted in Sinai and can still be seen there. The monastery was also a centre of attraction for monks from different Orthodox Churches. In addition to Greeks, St Catherine's was at various times inhabited by Slav and Georgian monks who brought their own artistic styles with them. Even Frankish monks lived in Sinai during the Crusades, and all left something of their art and culture behind. The monks have displayed their finest pieces in a small museum, so that visitors from the outside world can also see them.

The kafenion

After early Mass comes the nicest part of the day. Monks and visitors meet in the café, a light-flooded room situated not far from the church and modelled on a Greek kafenion. Upholstered benches line the walls, small tables are dotted around, and the walls are adorned with pictures of Greek and Russian monarchs and former abbots. Almost before I knew what was happening, I was thrust into the kafenion and handed a cup of hot tea. Pastries were served – there are always sweet things for breakfast – and tea, coffee and water dispensed. The atmosphere was relaxed and informal, but I understood little of what was said because the predominant language was Greek. I could now take a closer look at most of the residents of the Sinai monastery in the bright light of a winter's day in the desert. The monks wear black habits and black hats, which they seldom remove. The winter nights are cold, so many scarves and rough knitted jackets are worn beneath their robes. Nearly all the monks sport bushy beards, most of which overhang their chests. I learnt a little later that there were 22 monks in the monastery. Fourteen of them were currently assembled in the kafenion, the majority engaged in lively conversation. For the moment, they politely ignored me. I was plied with tea, coffee and pastries, but nobody asked me who I was or what I wanted.

At length I plucked up my courage and asked a young monk beside me whether the librarian, Father Justin, was present. 'That's Father Justin,' he said, indicating a big man sitting opposite me. A tall, gaunt figure with one of the longest beards in the kafenion, he had already caught my eye in the church, being one of the two alternate singers who had accompanied the Mass for hours from their lecterns. Father Justin more or less accorded with one's idea of a desert monk: a grave, pale-faced man with ascetic, almost ethereal features, he was probably little more than skin and bone beneath his habit. Delighted to have encountered the main reason for my precipitate trip to Sinai at the first opportunity, I went over to him, introduced myself, and thanked him for the invitation. His manner was friendly but aloof.

The monk seated beside him, one of the few who had been eyeing me curiously, butted in as soon as he gathered that my visit concerned Tischendorf, and that I was interested in the monks' opinion of the

German traveller in the East. 'Tischendorf was one of those arrogant Westerners who think we can't understand our own sacred texts,' he said, but Justin cut him short before he could really get going. The archbishop had reserved the personal right to explain the monastery's attitude towards Tischendorf to me, he said rather disapprovingly, so everyone else should refrain from doing so. This remark instantly sufficed to erect something akin to an invisible wall around me – one that was seldom breached in the ensuing days. A German journalist on the track of Constantin Tischendorf was clearly a hot potato. Father Justin suggested that we meet at the archbishop's residence at ten to discuss matters. He pointed out of the window at a building not far away. On that note, I was temporarily dismissed. Father Justin left the kafenion, which gradually emptied. With two hours' grace until ten, I at last had an opportunity to inspect the monastery.

The monastery precinct

At first sight, the whole precinct looked smaller than I had assumed from photographs, but this might have been partly because of the early hour. The monastery still lay in the shadow of the mountains, which thus looked nearer and more oppressive than they really are. When the sun had risen a little higher and I could survey St Catherine's and its environs from a terrace that enabled me to see over the top of the wall, the monastery's magnificent location became clearly visible. A big valley opens out to the west. Also on that side lies the magically beautiful monastery garden, whose palm and olive trees look green and luxuriant even in the middle of winter. Blossoming fruit trees reinforce the impression of almost unreal beauty because everything else around consists of bare, naked rock. The monastery is situated at the end of a valley like a cul-de-sac, although the mountains to the east are not very high and a little road runs over the summit. To the right and left of the monastery, by contrast, the mountainsides rise steeply. This exerts a powerful acoustic effect. Every sound can be heard for miles, and a flock of pigeons flying over the monastery sounds like someone shaking out wet laundry.

Seen from the garden, which is also traversed by the approach road leading to the monastery, Mount Sinai is on the right. The summit cannot be seen from the monastery because one's view is obstructed by its precipitous north flank. The first things that strike one inside the high defensive walls are two towers. One is the bell tower built on to the church in 1870. Immediately facing it is a minaret. This association with Islam in the midst of a Greek Orthodox monastery is said to date from the 10th century, when Caliph al-Hakim, reputedly an unpredictable mystic, threatened to attack the monastery. According to legend, the monks hurriedly set to work to build a minaret and convert the adjoining building, hitherto used as a hostel, into a mosque. When the Caliph's troops saw the mosque inside the monastery, they broke off the attack.

Although it cannot be historically established beyond doubt whether this really happened, the effect of having the mosque within its precincts has been, and still is, that the existence of the Greek Orthodox monastery, despite being surrounded by Islam since the 7th century, has never been seriously threatened. The monks even show visitors a *firman*, or handwritten edict from the Prophet Mohammed, who is said to have personally guaranteed the monastery's protection. However, since contact with the Christian world was often very sporadic in the centuries following the Arab conquest of Sinai, the Sinai monastery exists in a sort of time capsule. Both outwardly and in the mentality of its residents, the monastery is a relic of Byzantium. It is probable that the cultural essence of Byzantium has been better preserved in this little patch of desert than anywhere else in the world. Byzantine fortifications have protected the monastery until now, Byzantine art has remained preserved here for centuries, the monks' theological views do not essentially differ from those of their forebears, and their library contains treasures from the earliest days of Byzantium, which is why Tischendorf was so magically attracted to the monastery.

St Catherine's acquired its present appearance in the 1950s, when a large annexe with a central domed roof was erected on the northern defensive wall. This now houses the library, though its substructure was created in the 6th century. As Father Aaron had proudly told me in Cairo, the first hermits and other religiously-motivated settlers came to Sinai back in AD 180, in search of God's burning thorn bush.

After that, a small chapel and some primitive accommodation were built. The Sinaite monks and the Copts still argue over who was the real originator of monasticism. The first organized monasteries were founded by Coptic monks, but because they belonged to the patriarchate of Alexandria, they also belonged to the Orthodox Church. The monastic community in Sinai had its first claim to fame when, in far-off Byzantium, Constantine became the first Roman emperor to convert to Christianity, and his mother Helena, who became a fanatical believer in her old age, undertook an expedition to the oriental origins of her religion. In Jerusalem she promptly found the cross on which Jesus had died, and the Sinaite monks hastened to make her their patron saint. Allegedly because they were exposed to repeated Bedouin raids, Constantine's best-known successor, Emperor Justinian, acceded to the monks' written request to erect a church and, for their protection, the defensive walls that still stand today.

The monastery was, in fact, built as part of a defensive system that several of Justinian's predecessors had begun to develop on the Byzantine Empire's eastern frontier. Ultimately extending from Armenia to Egypt via Mesopotamia and Sinai, this was directed mainly against the Persian and Arab threat. Procopius of Caesarea, Justinian's court historian, reports in his work *De Aedificiis* that the fortress had served principally to fend off surprise attacks from the desert against Palestine. Of the founding of the monastery he wrote: 'A precipitous, terribly wild mountain, Sina by name, rises near the Red Sea. Living on this mountain are monks whose life is a kind of careful preparation for death. They enjoy solitude, which is very precious to them, without fear. Emperor Justinian built them a church, which he dedicated to the Mother of God, so that they can spend their lives in prayer and divine service. The emperor erected the church not on the summit of the mountain but much further down, it being impossible for anyone to spend the night on the summit because thunderclaps and other awesome manifestations of divine power, which strike terror into a person's body and soul, are to be heard there at night. It is said that Moses received the commandments from God in that place and announced them to his people. At the foot of the mountain the emperor erected a stout fortress and manned it with a strong military garrison, so that the barbaric Saracens could not surreptitiously invade Palestine proper from that region, which, as I already said, is unpopulated.'[4]

It is apparent from inscriptions on its timberwork that the church and the defensive walls enclosing it must all have come into being around 560. Why the monastery is called St Catherine's and not St Helena's or St Mary's, even though the monks originally invoked Helena, the emperor's mother, and Procopius records that Justinian subsequently dedicated the church to Mary the Mother of God, is down to a legend from later years. According to this, the bones of Catherine, a Christian martyr executed for her faith in Alexandria in the 10th century, were brought to Sinai by angels. These bones are now preserved in the monastery as relics, and the place has borne St Catherine's name ever since.

Although the monastery's walls of granite from Mount Sinai make a perfect architectural match for its surroundings, it has no social connection with them. Because of the Coptic Church's separation from the Orthodox mother church, there have for centuries been no indigenous Egyptian monks at St Catherine's. The monks continued to come from many parts of the empire until the fall of Byzantium; thereafter, however, the area from which the Sinai monastery drew its recruits narrowed to Mount Athos in northern Greece, Crete and Cyprus. To this day, St Catherine's Monastery is represented in both the latter islands by dependencies of its own. As a rule, the monks' first point of contact with the outside world is Cairo, whence communications are forwarded to Athens and on to Crete, Cyprus or Mount Athos.

The Bedouin

Suleyman was around 40 when I made his acquaintance, and a man of great experience. He knows the mountains of Sinai like the back of his hand, for he belongs to the Jebel or mountain tribe of Bedouin who have lived here for centuries. He has visited the tourist resorts on the Gulf of Aqaba and knows Cairo. He has learnt to read and write. Above all, though, in addition to his tribal dialect he speaks high Arabic, Greek and English. The last two languages he taught himself through contact with the outside world, for as Suleyman aptly remarks: 'I have no need to travel the wide world; the world comes to us.' And Suleyman has not let this opportunity slip. He has examined the world that came to him with an inquisitive eye, sought contact with it, and garnered experiences. His experiences have been predominantly good, which is why Suleyman is on good terms with the world.

The Fathers, as he calls the monks, 'are okay'. Some of them, whom he holds in particular esteem, even speak Arabic and take more interest in their surroundings than the rest. With the others he simply speaks Greek. That's okay too, because the Fathers are, after all, the reason why the Jebel, the mountain Bedouin, have done relatively well for centuries; moreover, the Bedouin have for centuries been the monks' link with their immediate surroundings. For as far back as the tribe can remember, the Jebel have always enjoyed a symbiotic relationship with the monastery. According to a legend which Suleyman himself propagates with great conviction, the Jebel came originally from Bosnia, the tribe's forefathers being Balkan soldiers whom Justinian stationed in Sinai during the 6th century for the monastery's protection. In the course of time they got together with Bedouin women and adopted Islam as the true faith – and that was how the Jebel tribe originated.

They guarded the monastery, kept it in touch with Cairo or Jerusalem by camel, and were supplied with food in return. The Bedouin no longer get grain from the monastery today, but those who work in the monastery itself, like Suleyman, are quite prosaically paid in money. In a certain sense, however, the tribe still enjoys a symbiotic relationship with the monastery, because on four days a week the peace and seclusion of St Catherine's are regularly and abruptly disturbed. This is when small proportions of the monastery precinct and the church are open to visitors from nine until twelve – and they fall on the artefact in the desert like swarms of locusts. Nearly all of them come from the seaside holiday resort of Sharm el Sheikh, whither they fly cheaply in chartered planes. They board their coaches there at 6.00 a.m. so as to be able to take at least a brief look behind the walls of the mysterious desert monastery. At sunrise a veritable serpent of air-conditioned coaches comes crawling along the narrow road to the monastery, to be greeted in a huge, sunlit square by the Bedouin. There is something special about this coach park: it was there that the tribes of Israel, while waiting for Moses, who was detained on the mountaintop by God for four weeks, are said to have cast their golden calf and worshipped their ancient idols. Today, thousands of visitors alight in this spot – seaside vacationers from Russia and Germany, from the Balkans, Italy and France. All are conducted from there to the monastery in groups, ushered into the interior of the fortress through a gate used only by tourists, and then taken on a round trip through the church, past the celebrated thorn bush, and into the small museum.

All this is organized by the Bedouin. They provide transport facilities with their camels; they act as tourist guides for those who want to see more than just the monastery's façade; they handle the sale of souvenirs and devotional objects; and they reliably extract the mass of humanity in time for midday service, so that by 12.30 p.m. the whole thing is over and nothing can be heard in the *wadi* but birds and monastery bells. 'Thanks to the tourists,' says Suleyman, 'our tribe is doing well. Many of us often earn ten dollars a day; workers in Cairo can only dream of such a sum.' There would be no tourists without the monastery. The Bedouin village now has mains water and an Egypt Telecom office from which it is technically possible to phone anywhere in the world, and a bus leaves for Cairo at six every morning. 'We can easily go there,' said Suleyman, 'but why should we? The city is noisy, overcrowded and dirty, and wages there are low.'

But there is another reason for the members of Sinai's 20 Bedouin tribes to avoid Cairo: they are regarded with suspicion elsewhere in Egypt. Suleyman is loath to talk about it, but Egyptian peasants find the nomads of the Sinai peninsula alien, even though most of them settled down long ago. Furthermore, a nationalistic factor has come into play since the Israeli occupation: the 'Bedus' are said to have got on too well with the Israelis. Suleyman himself has no distasteful memories of the years when the Israelis controlled Sinai. As a child he even learnt a smattering of Hebrew. 'Back then,' he says, 'the Jews considered building a synagogue on the summit of Mount Moses, where a chapel and a small mosque now stand. But they never got around to it.'

Suleyman did not learn his English from day-trippers or Orthodox pilgrims, however, but from the third group of visitors who regularly turn up at the monastery: professors of Byzantinist faculties at American or European universities, art historians, restorers, and the successors of Constantin Tischendorf, who conduct palaeographic research in the library. While I was at St Catherine's, a party of Italian architects was preparing to restore some buildings in the south-east corner of the precinct. Except with the Greeks, English is the lingua franca, so Suleyman gradually acquired his English by mixing with visitors from all over the world.

On one occasion, when I bumped into him in the local village, he proudly showed me his family home. All the villagers belong to the Jebel tribe, he told me, and they jealously defend their commercial interests against outside intrusion. 'Only members of our tribe can offer their services to tourists.' This connection with the Jebel Bedouin is still of advantage to the monks as well. The Bedouin form a sort of buffer between the monastery and its Islamic surroundings, and they keep the whole place going. Everything from gardening to cooking to building work is handled by the Bedouin. To this day, therefore, the monastery lives in a perfect symbiosis with the Jebel tribe from Bosnia.

The Archbishop

Shortly before ten I was standing expectantly outside the archbishop's residence. Father Justin appeared a little later, as promised, and we entered the building together. The first thing we came to was a reception hall, though 'hall' is something of an exaggeration. It was a largish room provided with chairs and cushions that might have seated some 20 people. Beyond this antechamber lay the archbishop's study. Justin intimated that I should wait for a moment while he had a word with the archbishop in private. A longish moment went by before he returned, shaking his head, and told me that the archbishop was indisposed. 'He's feeling very tired today and doesn't wish to receive visitors. He has instructed me what to tell you.'

In the photographs I had seen of His Holiness Archbishop Damianos, he was a man in his prime with a black moustache and beard devoid of a single white hair, but those pictures were taken almost 30 years ago. Today the archbishop is 75 years old and has for 35 of those years been the supreme authority of the autonomous Orthodox Church of Sinai, whose thousand or more members make it the smallest independent Orthodox Church of all. In order to keep his denomination above water, Damianos has to be not only a good monk but also a diplomat capable of steering his monastery through the perils of the world outside the walls of the desert fortress. During his term of office, Israeli troops captured Sinai and left it again. There was war in Cyprus when Turkish troops occupied part of the island, an act which the Greek Orthodox Church regards as the most heinous Turkish crime since the conquest of Constantinople.

Greece was afflicted with a fascist military dictatorship and later became a member of the European Union. The collapse of the Soviet Union signified a resurrection of Orthodoxy in Eastern Europe, in the Balkans and Russia, with the result that millions more people suddenly became active participants in the Orthodox cosmos. All these issues had and are still having repercussions on the remote desert monastery, and Archbishop Damianos has to deal with them. Above all, though, he is engaged in maintaining contact with local dignitaries and the competent ministers in Cairo. The day after our aborted meeting, for example, although in poor health, he visited the governor of Sinai to discuss matters affecting public utilities and restoration.

Otherwise than in Turkey, for example, where the state regards the Greek patriarchate with extreme suspicion and refuses to give Patriarch Bartholomew his due title, 'Ecumenical Patriarch', the Egyptians are glad to have the monastery in Sinai. It is good for tourism and beneficial to their international image for the Islamic state to show tolerance towards its Christian believers.

What is more complicated for the Sinaites is maintaining an internal Orthodox balance. Canonically speaking, the election of their archbishop has to be confirmed by the patriarchate in Jerusalem and Constantinople. Now that Russian Orthodoxy has regained strength, however, Russia is once more playing an important role, if only because more Russian than Greek pilgrims will soon be visiting the monastery. It was not surprising, therefore, that the light in

Archbishop Damianos's study usually burned for longer than in any other room, and that he could not always attend early Mass. It was not until my third day at the monastery that I suddenly spotted him leaving the church on his way to the kafenion. His once dark beard was now white and his back bent, and he clearly found it hard to manage the steps leading up to our breakfast venue. He was initially puzzled when I accosted him, but then I uttered the codeword Tischendorf. 'Ah, you're the German journalist who wants to write a book about Tischendorf, aren't you?' Although he was prepared to chat in the kafenion, he avoided the subject of Tischendorf in favour of Istanbul, which he visits regularly. Archbishop Damianos, I learnt, is a great friend of Patriarch Bartholomew.

This was rather strange, actually, because Bartholomew is widely regarded within the Orthodox hierarchy as overly liberal. A patriarch who worries about the world's ecological condition, warns of catastrophic climate change and is strongly committed to interfaith dialogue seems suspect to many in the Orthodox Church. Most of the Sinaite monks reject talks with the Catholic Church about the schism of 1054. 'The Orthodox Church,' Father Aaron said categorically, 'cannot recognize any other churches as of equal status. They are not orthodox – they seceded from us.' Talks such as those between Bartholomew and Pope Benedict XVI in Istanbul in the autumn of 2007 are regarded as highly suspect. 'In talks with the Catholic Church,' said Father Aaron, 'our bishops could fare exactly like the Byzantine emperors who sought a rapprochement with Rome. They held talks, but no one followed them.' Just as the majority of Byzantines during the final phase of the empire refused to make any concessions to Rome in return for support from the West and preferred to live under Ottoman rule, the monks of Sinai are against effacing the differences with Catholicism. Accepting the Pope as premier bishop of a united church would seem wholly unthinkable to them.

Practically speaking, there have been no theological disputes within Orthodoxy for over 1,000 years. 'Our foundation,' said Father Justin, 'is the seven councils of the then still united church.' Those seven councils were all organized from Byzantium; the last took place in 787 at Nicaea, the place where Constantine had convoked the first council more than four centuries earlier. The councils laid down the doctrine the Orthodox Church still regards as binding. All the subsequent debates in the Middle Ages that led, among other things, to the development of Protestantism, not to mention the controversies about the Enlightenment leading to historico-critical research into the life of Jesus and the historical relevance of biblical texts, which Tischendorf opposed, are entirely alien to the Orthodox Church and have never taken place within it. In the monastic community of Sinai they tend to be entirely ignored. 'Why,' asked Father Justin, 'should we worry about the historical Jesus? Isn't it enough that he's the Son of God?'

The monastery's reference library contains a 6th-century book which Archbishop Damianos extols in an enthusiastic foreword as a guide to monastic virtue and piety. This is *Climax, or the Ladder to Heaven*, a theological handbook by St John of Sinai, a hermit who lived in a cave and was later appointed abbot of the Sinai monastery. In that capacity he wrote a didactic work for the monks of his own house and of an affiliated monastery. In it he describes the 30 steps that lead straight to celestial bliss.

The German edition I came across in the Sinai monastery is by a monk named Georgis Makedos, who lives in a monastery on Mount Athos but previously spent a long time in Germany and translated the old Greek text into German after his return.

The individual steps to bliss described by St John are entitled, *inter alia,* 'On renouncing a vain way of life', 'On mildness and gentleness', and 'On the imperishability of chastity'. According to the translator, the treatise, which was originally written on parchment, consists of 'spiritual remarks, theological and ascetic ideas, anthropological and psychological observations. Everything stems from his [John's, J.G.] personal experience of the spiritual battle, his perspicacity, and his way of life in Christ.'

In his foreword, Archbishop Damianos writes: 'John was and is a great spiritual teacher.' For this reason he is celebrated in the Orthodox Church as an important spiritual and moral personality and one of its authentic teachers, not only on the date of his death, 30 March, but on the fourth Sunday in Lent. It is also noteworthy that, in accordance with ancient custom, his eternally new, profound and edifying text is read aloud in Orthodox monasteries.

Archbishop Damianos describes him as being a great spiritual leader to this day. Said to have been originally from Constantinople, John spent the bulk of his life alone in a cave almost two days' march from the monastery. He was a hermit and ascetic. This 'spiritual immersion in God' has remained the ideal of the Sinaite monks, the last Byzantines, to this day.

Through the Desert

Tischendorf traverses Sinai in the footsteps of Moses

It may have been about two hours after quitting the manna tamarisks that I saw probably the most magnificent sight I had ever beheld in my life. We were riding up a gentle slope: on both sides the rocks drew closer and closer. Suddenly, we were confronted by two colossal, smooth granite walls that rose perpendicularly into the air – a majestic structure! They are like petrified palm trees melted into one mass, brown, grey and red; irregular streaks of a dark blue steel colour undulate downwards as if lightning had thereby traced its fiery course. It is a portal as if to the throne of the Lord of Lords.

I was silent and astounded. 'Here is holy ground,' was my feeling: here has the angel of God held sway, to arrest the human eye for some great purpose. We rode through the portal; we rode upwards as if over invisible steps: the walls of rock drew apart. We were standing in an open space covered with vegetation, enclosed like an amphitheatre and punctuated only by solitary boulders resembling Areopagites.

In the midst of these impressions I thought I heard bells chiming in the distance: this consummated the festal sensation. I had not heard a bell for months: now they suddenly rang out like sweet and suppressed but painful memories. When I raised the subject with my dragoman, he replied, almost derisively, 'There are no bells here.' Nevertheless, we were in fact near the remarkable Jebel Nakus, or Bell Mountain, which, because of the bell-like notes it gives out when a footstep traverses its loose sand, has led to the belief that a monastery lies buried beneath it.

As we emerged from this amphitheatre the road resumed its previous sublime character: directly ahead of me was a veritable triumphal way; there, communing with the clouds in solemn majesty, stood the peaks of Sinai.[1]

A 19th-century photograph of the Pharain Oasis.

When Tischendorf and his companions reached the granite triumphal arch, he had been traversing the desert for 11 days. All of his research in Cairo had directed him to one particular place: St Catherine's Monastery in the Sinai Desert and its celebrated library of ancient manuscripts. In Cairo, in addition to his dragoman Ali and his personal interpreter and guide, a 25-year-old Egyptian from Giza, he had hired three Bedouin and four camels to form the little expeditionary force that was to escort him to the monastery of the Sinaite Brothers in the midst of the mountainous wilderness in the south of the Sinai Peninsula. After some lengthy haggling outside the gates of the Austrian Embassy, whose experts assisted Tischendorf in negotiating with the Bedouin, they eventually agreed on a sum which the tight-fisted Saxon considered favourable and set off the following Monday. Constantin Tischendorf, who was riding a camel for the first time in his life, rejoiced at how convenient and safe it was up there, and how comfortably one could sit for long periods on this 'ship of the desert'. He began to see himself arriving at the Sinai monastery almost as soon as his little caravan left the gates of Cairo behind, but he soon discovered that the desert had different ordeals in store than a journey by stagecoach from Leipzig to Paris. The first thing he suffered from was the sun. It wasn't that he hadn't already sweated and groaned in Cairo, but there was no shade out in the desert and no escaping into cool interiors. He had donned a straw hat and, on the advice of an acquaintance in Cairo, draped his face and neck in a silk cloth. This, so his friend had insisted, would save him from returning with a complete 'facial metamorphosis'. He also took with him a small tent in which he proudly spent *the first night in my own house*. In other respects he rode and walked with the lightest of baggage. His principal items of equipment were a few cooking utensils, a few blankets, and a large number of waterskins.

But 12 May, the day he set out, was not far off the Egyptian summer, and the summer proved to be murderously hot. His journey turned out accordingly. Tischendorf later described the details in a letter to his brother: *I always set off early, at sunrise. From ten or eleven until four or five o'clock I rested, partly for a midday meal, partly for repose; then we continued on our way until eleven or twelve at night. I was en route for twelve long days; on the fourth day we were in Suez; we also passed only three Bedouin villages, naught else but desert, almost always enclosed in a river valley of varying width. Because I had believed the journey would be far shorter, my cuisine was not plentiful. Our chickens and pigeons, our rice, our cheese, some preserves, tea and coffee – that was just about all.*

At night I always slept in the open. [He only pitched his tent against the sun during the day. J.G.] *A sheepskin, my fur and a big woollen blanket formed the bed. You can understand how easily one of the very common venomous snakes, whose bite mostly proves lethal after a few hours, can crawl up to you. We killed two such snakes, which, when the Bedouin see them, are greeted with cries of fear, one of them with two pistol shots. Few wild animals were in evidence; I saw a wild pig and a wolf very close to us, we often heard wolves howling, and one morning we found the tracks of a tiger near our sleeping quarters. Ants and flies gave us a lot of trouble.*

At about twelve on the second night we wearily lay down. Near me the three Bedouin, nearer still my dragoman; I myself flanked by my trunk, by our long travelling basket, and covered with a woollen blanket; right beside me my heavily loaded, double-barrelled shotgun. Several hours after dozing off I woke up: above me the beautiful, starry sky, beside me the sleeping Arabs, in the distance the grazing, bellowing camels; added to which, I was in the middle of the fearsome desert. You will readily understand that, in such circumstances, you have to believe in your lucky star or, rather, in your guardian angel, to be able to go calmly back to sleep.[2]

Being young, adventurous and ambitious, however, Tischendorf soon became inured to his novel situation. What helped him above all was an idea. On his way across Sinai, he believed, he was treading in the very footsteps of Moses, who had allegedly led his people out of Egypt and into the Promised Land of Canaan. On reaching Suez he had his tent pitched on a hill from which he could look out to sea and noted: *So this was where the Lord's strong arm was revealed! The waters roar; they still tell the sacred old story.*[3]

Tischendorf went nearly all the way to the Sinai monastery with Bible in hand, so as to discover the places named in Exodus during the flight of the tribes of Israel. He identified the ford the tribes must, in his opinion, have used south of Suez; he overnighted at the Springs of Moses; he thought he had found the oasis at which Moses rested with his people; and, last but not least, he sampled manna, the food reported to have fallen from the sky when the refugees started to complain of their poor diet. Tischendorf did, of course, believe that the exodus from Egypt was a historical event; he merely disputed with other historians and biblical scholars over the exact route Moses took. He was, however, prepared to concede that God had also made use of nature in accomplishing his miracles.

On intimate terms with Moses

Although survey work for the breakthrough from the Mediterranean to the Red Sea had already been undertaken when Tischendorf reached Suez in 1844, almost two decades would elapse before work on the canal began. (It was excavated between 1859 and 1869.) Consequently, his little caravan crossed the Red Sea exactly as people had done just under 3,000 years earlier, that is to say, by way of a ford that was readily passable at low tide, especially when a strong east wind forced the water back. *The water at no point came up to the camels' bellies*, he himself stated.[4] So it was not essential for God to have parted the waters to enable the Israelites to pass and then engulf Pharaoh's army; they could have got across the strait at low tide without his assistance, and it was still more improbable that an Egyptian army would have ridden into the incoming tide. After all, the Egyptians had been crossing the Red Sea for centuries in order to exploit the mines in southern Sinai.

The exodus from Egypt, the tribes' 40-year trek across Sinai and their entry into the Promised Land to the sound of the trumpets that demolished the walls of Jericho are just as much of an Old Testament myth as the burning bush with which God manifested himself to Moses and the handover of the Ten Commandments on Mount Sinai.

The fact is, archaeologists have never yet come across any evidence of Israelite tribes in Egypt, let alone any reports of the flight of 600,000 warriors – counting their families, some 2 million people, as it says in the Bible – or of the destruction of a pursuing Egyptian army. Whether or not there ever was an exodus of proto-Israelite tribes from Egypt is the subject of scholarly debate. The only contemporary sources are Egyptian, and they are not very informative. Most biblical scholars assume that the exodus of the Semitic tribes should be dated circa 1300 BC, in the reign of either Ramses II or his successor Merenptah. A stele of Merenptah is said to refer to hostilities between the Egyptians and Israelite tribes. Others, citing the Bible, date these events 150 years earlier. It is likeliest, however, that a mass departure of Israelite tribes as described in Exodus never took place, and that the exodus story is an ideal summarization of the long-term occupation of Canaan by Semites returning from Egypt – a legend that has become Israel's foundation myth.

In the centuries before Ramses there was a continuous exchange of populations between the Near East and Egypt. For one thing, Semites attracted by the wealth of Egypt infiltrated the land around the Nile almost like illegal immigrants; for another, various pharaohs brought back prisoners from military campaigns east of Sinai and installed them in Egypt as slaves. Finally, there were the Hyksos. It is possible that the essence of the myth relates to their history. The Hyksos were a Semitic tribe from Canaan, probably Amurrites, who emigrated to Egypt around 1700 BC, settled in the Nile Delta and founded Avaris, a capital of their own. In the 16th century BC they even, during a weak phase in the Egyptian pharaonic dynasty, seized power on the Upper Nile. They are said to have imported horses into Egypt and introduced the chariot, then the most modern form of military technology. In around 1530 BC, however, Pharaoh Ahmose defeated them in a major battle and drove them back to Palestine from the Nile. For this reason, many scholars associate the Hyksos with the legend of the exodus from Egypt, particularly as it is not altogether clear, even in the legend, whether it was an organized withdrawal, an expulsion, or a thoroughgoing flight.

But the exodus story may also relate to nameless immigrants coming into Egypt. The east of the Nile Delta was repeatedly infiltrated, because of its fertility, by Semitic tribes from across the Sinai Desert. However, these immigrants were invariably expelled as soon as a strong Egyptian central authority established itself. This may also have been the case in the time of Ramses II (1303–1213 BC). He built his capital, Ramses City, more or less on the site of the Hyksos' Avaris, and it was from there, according to the Bible, that the Israelites' exodus began. In fact, successive Semitic immigrants were expelled over a period of several hundred years after the fall of the Hyksos – a process subsequently compressed into a great story in the myth of the exodus from Egypt.

Nevertheless, the royal capital in which the Old Testament states that Moses was exposed in an 'ark of bulrushes' and found by a princess of the pharaonic court did exist. The long-lost city was buried beneath desert sand, having been looted and destroyed thousands of years ago. Manfred Bietak, director of the Austrian Archaeological Institute in Cairo, excavated Ramses City in the 1990s.[5] The alluvial land of the Nile Delta in north-east Egypt is said to have been the location one of the largest pharaonic cities, in which the kings of the 19th and 20th dynasties reigned. The best-known of these was Ramses II himself, one of the greatest builders in Egyptian history, who developed the city on a site covering as much as ten square kilometres. But the city had vanished almost without trace, which is what makes excavation so difficult. Only the lowest tiers of foundations can still be identified. Everything else was destroyed, removed or buried in drifting sand. There is no trace of any Israelite tribes. The city was probably abandoned when the arm of the Nile that supplied it with water became silted up and dried out. Archaeologists conjecture that it was transferred to Tanis, 25 kilometres to the north, where royal tombs of the 21st and 22nd dynasties have been found. Tanis is an impressive expanse of ruins, even today, and most of its columns, obelisks, temples and colossal statues were probably brought there from Ramses City when Tanis superseded it.

At all events, it was from Ramses City that the Israelites were said to have fled in the time of the great pharaoh, or between 1303 and 1213 BC. One can visualize a gigantic column of people, a regular mass migration, debouching into the desert on the pretext of celebrating a religious festival. The journey to the Promised Land purportedly took 40 years, although it could have been completed in four months.

But none of this threw Constantin Tischendorf in the least. That God, in the course of the plagues he visited on the pharaoh to extract his consent to the Israelites' departure, should have allowed all the male infants in Egypt to be put to death, Tischendorf, in common with all biblical fundamentalists, considered not only historically true but a good deed. The same applied to the annihilation of the Egyptian army in the waters of the Red Sea: *I will sing unto the Lord, for he hath triumphed gloriously; the horse and his rider hath he thrown into the sea,* he wrote in his diary, quoting the Bible. *The Lord shall reign for ever and ever. This triumphal song of the chosen servant of God* [Moses, J. G.] *will, as long as there is history and faith in the world, hover faithfully and for ever over the passage of the Israelites through the Red Sea.*[6]

After Tischendorf himself and his Bedouin had crossed the Red Sea – he in a boat belonging to the consul for Austria and France in Suez, a Greek named Kosta – they camped for the first night on the Sinai side by the so-called Springs of Moses. The water looked rather milky – doubtless not up to German standards of purity – but was drinkable. This is where the Israelites were said to have called their first halt and given thanks to God for their deliverance after safely crossing the sea. Tischendorf dwelt in two worlds during his journey. On the one hand there were the hardships of his trek across the desert, his fear of being attacked, and the minor disasters *en route* (the wind blew off his straw hat and sun veil, and the Bedouin had to spend hours searching for them); on the other, there was the fantasy world of the Bible into which Tischendorf was continually escaping, as his journal testifies: *We had proceeded along the Garandel Valley for about an hour before we came to the fountain and the little stream that hurries toward the sea. It is a magnificent oasis; where we rested, it lay like a jewel enclosed by cliffs of limestone. We waded for a long time through reeds as tall as ourselves. Tamarisks and low palms wound like a garland from east to west. Notwithstanding the intensity of the sun's rays concentrated in this beautiful valley, so that even the least refreshment was difficult to obtain and the water of the fountain itself tasted warm, I was overwhelmed by the thought that we were in the Elim of the Bible, the Elim where there were twelve wells of water and three score and ten palm trees. Elim had always attracted me; it had delighted me to think of the children of Israel refreshing themselves beneath these palms and by these gladsome wells after their exhausting journey across barren, sandy desert. So I rested long and happily today in this blessed valley. Toward evening, however, contrary to their usual custom, the*

Bedouin urged that we move on, fearing that their camels would be bitten by insects.[7]

The stop after Elim was Wadi Pharain, or 'Feiranthal', as Tischendorf calls it. This *wadi* begins at the Red Sea and runs east for several kilometres like an immense gorge between the mountains of Sinai, which grow steadily higher. Just as it was 3,000 years ago, the *wadi* is the only route to the Promised Land, and even today the motorway runs inland from the sea to St Catherine's Monastery on Mount Sinai. When Tischendorf and his Bedouin entered the Wadi Pharain, he followed a path that led eventually to a Bedouin village in the Pharain Oasis. Although delighted by the tall date palms growing there, he pressed on further into the adjoining Sheikh Valley, for it was there that he went in search of manna.

I rejoiced exceedingly that I had entered the valley at the beginning of the season at which the formation of manna takes place. The months of June and July are considered to be this period; and I roamed eagerly from branch to branch, trying to discover by eye what was so apparent from the smell. How happy I was on soon finding, on many branches of one of the tallest and largest shrubs, what resembled shiny beads or condensed drops of dew. I broke off some of the finest of them, for I felt convinced that my hands were indeed holding manna in the process of formation. This thickish substance was sticky and emitted the same strong smell as the shrub. I tasted it, and the flavour, to the extent that I can find a comparison, most closely resembles that of honey. [...]

But what lends this manna of the Sheikh Valley such great interest is the recollection of the heavenly bread that fed the Israelites in the desert. And whatever may be objected to the comparison of the one with the other, I am nevertheless convinced that the manna of the Sheikh Valley has a special and close relationship with Biblical manna, for this region coincides with the region where the Israelites first received manna.[8]

As a child of his time confronted by criticism of the historicity of Bible stories, Tischendorf did also concede that his manna could not be the same as the one described in the Bible. *There are enough varieties of it, admittedly. The biblical manna fell from the sky during the night and, in the morning, lay on the fields like dew. Moreover, it was capable of sustaining an army of two million for forty years. [...] Admittedly, the tamarisk manna of Sinai seems diminished in importance by this, especially as, in the case of the Israelites' manna, one must not overlook the miracle. But does not the miracle retain its true character when we conceive of today's manna being deducible on every side, by divine grace, from the former food of the Israelites? Were it not seemingly too far-fetched, I would say that the vapour rising from the tamarisk groves might very readily fall back to earth as dew. This idea may be at least as admissible as the supposition that the present manna appears to be a feeble after-effect of the biblical bread of heaven.*[9]

The problem with monks

But Tischendorf had little time left in which to ponder the relationship between biblical and modern manna, because he was steadily approaching the goal of his trek across the desert. There was an outpost of the Sinai monastery at the Pharain Oasis, and less than a day's march separated the Sheikh Valley from St Catherine's. After one last night in the desert, which he spent as guest of a Bedouin tribe, Tischendorf set off at dawn on the final stage of his journey.

The morning was pleasantly cool. I was particularly struck today by the difference in temperature I had already felt in the last two days. To be sure, the Sheikh Valley, where we now were, is several thousand feet higher than the Garandel Valley [biblical Elim, J.G.], where the heat was insupportable. I did not see the monastery until we were in its immediate vicinity; it is situated in a long but narrow valley between the Mountain of St Epistemius, also called Jebel el Deir, and Horeb [modern Mount Sinai or Mount Moses, J.G.]. However, its presence is most agreeably heralded by its splendid garden, which, complete with cypresses, pomegranates and orange trees, peers forth amiably from among its grey stone walls. Because of these walls, which are nigh on forty feet high, the monastery itself resembles a miniature fortress. This impression is still further reinforced by the lack of an entrance proper. The door opening, to which one has to be winched by rope, is thirty feet up. Several Bedouin had gathered beneath this door before I got there. They did not neglect to announce my arrival by shouting and firing their guns.[10]

And so, after 12 arduous days in the desert, Tischendorf at last stood in front of the monastery's lofty walls, fervently hoping that the monks would let him in – or rather, haul him up. He was not entirely confident of this, because another German scholar, who had sought admission a few years earlier, was compelled to remain outside on the grounds that he had no letter of recommendation from the Sinaites in Cairo. Although Tischendorf had obtained one from the Sinaite monastery in Cairo, he was reluctant to produce it because it stated that 'the German' could be admitted but was to be kept away from the library. He later described this dilemma to his brother as follows: *A letter from the president of the monastery in Cairo became unusable from my point of view because that perfidious Greek instructed his monastery to place everything at my disposal but be wary of me in respect of the manuscripts.*[11] For that reason, he had obtained two further letters in Suez from Kosta, the consul there, and a man named Manoli, the monastery's supplier. These he placed in the basket which the monks, who were looking down at him suspiciously from their hole in the wall, had lowered for the purpose. However, they had already learnt via the Bedouin's mysterious channels of communication that he had applied to their brothers in Cairo and obtained a letter of recommendation from them.

Where was this letter? they demanded from above, and Tischendorf had to resort to a white lie. Alas, said their German visitor, he had inadvertently left that important letter, together with many other documents, behind in Cairo. Tischendorf correctly surmised that the monks did not really buy this excuse. *Although my information may not have been altogether satisfactory, they no longer forbore to haul me up by rope into their cheerful sanctuary.* Once up there, he found himself surrounded by *grave-faced men in black robes*. He was greeted by the Superior, the head of the monastery, a man, he wrote, *whose gaze, notwithstanding the delicacy of his features, conveys the strongest impression of duplicity.*[12]

An audacious verdict indeed from someone who had just wangled admission to the monastery by means of a lie! For someone whose life's work was dependent upon the cooperation of the Greek Orthodox monks in both Sinai and Cairo, and who would strive for decades to persuade those same monks to approve the publication of his great find, Tischendorf's language was extremely derogatory and

In the 19th century, visitors were winched up to the monastery entrance. Tischendorf himself had to persuade the monks to haul him up by producing letters of recommendation.

condescending. No wonder the monks in Cairo wished to warn their brothers at St Catherine's against too trustingly permitting Tischendorf to root around in their ancient library. In his initial encounters with oriental Christians, the man from Leipzig had proved himself lacking in sensitivity.

Tischendorf was so obsessed with his mission to find the original version of the Bible that he took it for granted that everyone he had to deal with was equally convinced of the essential nature of his project. He was confirmed in this attitude by reactions to his decipherment of the Codex Ephraemi in Paris. His articles in the *Augsburger Allgemeine* were devoured not only by the educated German and Austrian middle class; the German and Austrian nobility were also fascinated by the idea of finding the genuine books of the Apostles. The search for the original version of the Bible aroused public enthusiasm similar to that surrounding the excavations of ancient civilizations in Mesopotamia or attempts to decipher the secrets of the Pyramids in Egypt. The Orient formed the screen upon which European romantics projected their yearnings. Babylon, Jerusalem, Troy and the Pyramids were mystical places that whetted people's imaginations and made it seem possible that the original version of the Scriptures might have been left behind in the East by God.

So Constantin Tischendorf had no inhibitions about enlisting representatives of the European powers on behalf of his project. Almost his first step on arrival in Cairo had been to contact the Austrian envoy. Neither Saxony nor any of the other small German states was diplomatically represented in Egypt, so the embassy of the Danubian monarchy was the logical place to start. It is probable that the Austrian envoy, Consul-General von Laurin, was under instructions from Vienna because the imperial court had also taken an interest in the Codex Ephraemi, and he did not hesitate to place himself at the young Leipziger's disposal. Only the day after he arrived, Tischendorf was able to ride to Shubra, the residence of the Viceroy of Egypt, accompanied by the Austrian consul-general. Officially, Egypt was still a part of the Ottoman Empire ruled by the Sultan in Constantinople, but the viceroy had already gained so much autonomy that in practice he did as he pleased and was answerable to the Sultan as a matter of form only. The viceroy, Mehmet Ali, was one of the most remarkable of oriental potentates. He had originally come to Egypt as a junior officer in the Ottoman army at the beginning of the 19th century, when the Sultan's authority was already little more than formal. Shortly before, in 1799, Napoleon had fought the famous campaign in the wake of which a sizeable number of European scholars had visited Egypt and written detailed accounts of that mysterious country on the Nile. Although the French were then defeated by the British, tactical considerations of British colonial policy dictated that the Ottoman Sultan's formal authority be preserved and that London pursue its interests in the background. Into this vacuum stepped Mehmet Ali.

With immense brutality but great diplomatic skill, he succeeded in fighting his way to the top of the Egyptian administration, tolerated and courted by Britain and France as well as Constantinople. Mehmet Ali is regarded as Egypt's first modernizer. The country had slumbered on the periphery of the Ottoman Empire since its conquest by Selim at the beginning of the 16th century. With the appearance of the European powers and its growing detachment from the Sultan's steadily disintegrating empire, Egypt regained its status as an independent historical entity. Although the Suez Canal had yet to be built, the country already played an important role for the British in its capacity as a turntable on the way to India.

Tischendorf was most impressed by his visit to the venerable viceroy in Shubra. Above all, though, he received Mehmet Ali's permission to move around the country in complete freedom. Without hesitation, he made straight for his goal. At various meetings within the German and Austrian community in Cairo he had learnt that the Greek Orthodox patriarch of Alexandria, who often spent time in Cairo, was reputed to be guarding an exceptional bibliophilic treasure. The patriarch had walled up hundreds of manuscripts, a whole library never yet seen by any expert. All these manuscripts reportedly came from Antioch, one of the most important Christian cities of the first two centuries AD, where Peter himself is said to have headed a community and whence he set out on his successful missionary journeys. To Tischendorf, therefore, a treasury of manuscripts from Antioch seemed like a Promised Land of his own. In company with the Austrian consul-general, who was personally acquainted with the patriarch, he set off as soon as possible for Old Cairo, the Christian quarter.

But Tischendorf's meeting with the patriarch was a disaster. He describes the 91-year-old dignitary as vain, arrogant and intellectually out of his depth. His attire, for example, was more sumptuous than the Pope's. Tischendorf might have overlooked this oriental splendour had he gained access to the library, but the patriarch first insisted on satisfying himself that his visitor knew Greek. He made him read aloud from a work by St John Chrysostom, which Tischendorf did poorly. The patriarch declared that his reading was no great shakes as yet. The old man was equally unimpressed by some polite remarks which Tischendorf delivered in Greek. *He harshly castigated the least slip in my modern Greek pronunciation,* Tischendorf complained later. *It seemed that the patriarch had the sensitive ear of a Parisian socialite.*

The patriarch was now even less inclined to have his library wall knocked down so that Tischendorf could examine the manuscripts inside, nor could the Austrian consul-general prevail on him to do so. When the latter explained at length that Tischendorf was a great German scholar who had made it his task *to examine the ancient codices of the original New Testament text with his own eyes, in order to derive from their compilation a text that would be as close as possible to the Apostles' own writings,* the patriarch merely made a weary, dismissive gesture. 'We have all we need,' he replied. 'We have the Gospels, we have the Apostles; what more do we require?'

Resignedly, Tischendorf noted: *The concept of criticism may have been ringing in his ears for the first time in his ninety-one years. He was dubious and suspicious of our explanations. Finally, he also argued that the library was walled up and could only be opened at great expense, to which we rejoined that we would be happy to bear the cost. Despite this, he made only a semblance of concurring, and we soon took our leave of him.*[13]

Tischendorf's whole dilemma is apparent from this first meeting with a senior Orthodox Christian. His request was totally incomprehensible, not only to the aged patriarch of Alexandria but also to the monks of St Catherine's Monastery in Sinai and those of the Coptic monasteries he visited, who could not understand what the

19th-century novices.

German was really after. The Orthodox Church and the other oriental Christian churches had ceased to debate the 'true doctrine' centuries earlier. No one had shaken their theological foundations since the 7th ecumenical council in 787, so it would never have occurred to any Orthodox priest or monk to question the biblical texts that had been used for centuries by the Byzantine Church. What mattered was devotion to God, which was a matter of the heart and of spiritual profundity, not of the intellect.

Tischendorf was horrified the first time he attended a service in the Sinaite monastery in Cairo. *All the brothers were in the chapel when we reached the Greek monastery of the Sinaites in Cairo, so we attended divine service too. There was an abundance of candlelight. The singing [...] was so absurdly discordant that the choirboys could scarcely suppress their laughter. How depressed one feels on leaving such a service. The Kyrie eleison, repeated countless times, enframes the whole ceremony.*[14]

Tischendorf describes early Mass in a Coptic monastery outside

Cairo in similar terms. *Before sunrise the little bell rang for Mass, which lasted over three hours. The readings from the Bible were partly Coptic, partly Arabic. What was sung struck me as very discordant. The Kyrie eleison and the Hallelujah were often repeated. I found the service extremely poor. The reader was spoken to in the midst of reading, and he responded. Someone began in the wrong place, someone else corrected him, and the correction was goodhumouredly accepted. Nevertheless, the Copt accompanying me was thoroughly earnest and reverent. After reading or recognizing whom it represented, he not only knelt before each icon but prostrated himself until his forehead touched the ground. He performed the same ceremony on entering the church.*[15]

A 19th-century ethnologist would doubtless have used the same language about some ritual performed by an unknown African tribe. On the one hand, the educated German; on the other, the oriental savage. Tischendorf's attitude towards his oriental Christian brothers became even more pronounced when his real objective, ancient early Christian manuscripts, was at issue.

Having at first, to his great annoyance, failed to persuade the Alexandrian patriarch to open his walled-up library – he was only later sent a few of its texts for inspection through the good offices of some acquaintances – Tischendorf devoted himself to the library of the Sinaites in Cairo. Not that there could be any talk of a library, judging by Tischendorf's description, for the monastery boasted only two cupboards stuffed with books and manuscripts.

The libraries in these monasteries, Tischendorf lamented, *are purely decorative; they occupy the place taken in our case by women's knick-knack tables.* In one cupboard he found some old Greek manuscripts that the monks were unable to read, and of whose existence they had allegedly been unaware. *To them, an ancient manuscript was a total novelty; they seemed to be acquainted with such things by reputation only, for no sooner had they learnt from me of their wealth of manuscripts than they also dreamt of their inestimable value.*[16]

Both in Cairo and later on, in Coptic monasteries, Tischendorf came to the conclusion that all the libraries were in a disastrous condition and quite unused as well. *The manuscripts repose beneath and on top of each other; lying covered in masses of dust on the floor and in big baskets are innumerable fragments of torn and damaged manuscripts,*[17] he complained of the library in one Coptic monastery. Moreover, in his opinion none of the monks was capable of reading the ancient manuscripts in Greek or Coptic. *Notwithstanding this,* he lamented, *their mistrust renders it very difficult, despite the poverty that surrounds them, to persuade them to sell their manuscripts.*[18] In short, the orientals were not only ignorant of what they possessed but unwilling to part with it.

No wonder, therefore, that the Sinaites in Cairo wanted to warn their brothers at St Catherine's against Tischendorf, for on this, his first trip to Egypt, the young Saxon still had no understanding of the lives of others in the far-off Orient.

The Sacred Mountain
Where God is very near

Seen at close quarters, the Bible's sacred mountain does not at first look particularly impressive. The wall of rock that confronts one is steep but not insurmountable, even by an inexperienced climber. For days I eyed that mountainside from the monastery terrace and wondered if I, at 50-plus, would make it to the top. I was determined to do so, because the alternative would be a long, roundabout track reportedly laid by an Egyptian pasha who preferred to be carried in a litter rather than toil up the steps of Mount Moses on foot. Ought I to take the pasha's track? Father Justin clinched the matter by telling me that the steps were the only authentic route up the mountain; besides, they were far more varied and attractive than the track, which was also a camel trail. So I took the steps, but they were not just 30 steps like those of St John's stairway to heaven. The route to Moses' heaven is said to number 3,700 steps. The monks of Sinai hewed them out of the rock back in the 4th century as an aid to reaching the summit, the very spot where God handed Moses the Ten Commandments from out of the cloud, and where they intended to erect a small chapel.

I did not count to see if there really are 3,700 steps, but they are certainly very numerous. Most of them are not steps in the sense of stairs. It probably took the monks decades of backbreaking work to cut ledges into projecting rocks to serve as steps for climbers. The 3,700-step route begins only a few hundred metres from the monastery walls. Although some of it winds upwards in tight spirals, most stretches head straight up the mountainside without any major detours. It is hard to picture Moses scrambling up there with the oldest and wisest members of the tribes of Israel.

Anyone using the Old Testament as a navigational aid might well

At this point, monks ascending Mount Sinai used to have to make confession before they could enter the mountain's sacred precinct.

have chosen some eminence other than Mount Horeb. Jebel Serbal overlooking the Pharain Oasis, for example, presents a considerably more majestic appearance, and that oasis in southern Sinai is the only place where a sizeable body of people could have lingered because of its unique access to water. Even in the immediate vicinity of Mount Sinai, Jebel Katarina's 2,640 metres render it 400 metres higher and a definite competitor for the site of Moses' encounter with God, because it would be only logical for that meeting to have taken place on the highest peak in Sinai.

Despite this, hermits and pilgrims disseminated the view, even in the 4th century, that this rugged, 2,300-metre-high mountain was the scene of the dramatic handover of the written covenant between God and his chosen people. Surprisingly enough, far less fuss is made about this place by the Jews, whom the covenant of Mount Sinai affects far more directly, than by Christian pilgrims from all over the world. Even during the years when Sinai was occupied by Israel, Jewish interest remained within bounds. On the other hand, remarkable numbers of Christians set off every year in order, once in their life, to stand on the spot where God came closer to a human being than anywhere else in the world. It has therefore become customary, not only for devout Christians but for hippies in search of a unique spiritual experience, to spend a night on the summit, where they can really savour to the full the sensation of proximity to God and, at dawn, watch the sun rise above the desert's mountain gorges.

One member of the second category was Carlos from Venezuela. Towards noon, when I reached the summit feeling thoroughly exhausted, he was warming his bones in the midday sun in a hollow sheltered from the wind. Nights on the summit are bitterly cold, especially in winter, but Carlos was such an enthusiast, he planned to spend at least one more night up there. The Bedouin have consequently made a business out of renting blankets for the night. Several wooden huts have sprung up just below the summit. These not only purvey tea and coffee but supply thick camelhair blankets and even tents, although there is hardly room on the summit to pitch one. Carlos claimed he was quite comfortable and not at all cold with two blankets, although the tip of his nose still looked rather red. He had stayed awake all night, he said, and had experienced a 'weird feeling'.

The way up Mount Sinai. The route is comparatively easy at first.

Settling down not far from Carlos was a group of Russian pilgrims I had overtaken on the last third of the climb: three men and two women who had only just managed to reach the summit. Once there, they unpacked their Bibles and food and looked around for a place to pray because the chapel, which was built 80 years ago out of the ruins of the little 4th-century church, was shut. A tiny 12th-century mosque has also found room on the summit beside it, which is why I was greeted at the top of Mount Sinai by the *ezan,* or imam's midday call to prayer – a greeting the Russian pilgrims at first found rather disconcerting. A little later, however, they found a small nook under a rocky spur that goes by the name of 'Moses' Cave', allegedly the place where the prophet waited for 40 days for God to manifest himself. But the pious pilgrims of today are clearly anxious to communicate, not only with God, but with their dear ones back home. One of the Russian women tried out her mobile phone and actually got a signal for a few seconds. Her voice broke with emotion as she trumpeted her triumphant news.

Things were rather more peaceful when Constantin Tischendorf reached the summit 165 years earlier. Having climbed the mountain accompanied only by his dragoman, he compared Mount Sinai with two other climbs he had made in previous years.

Some years ago, when I stood on the Rigi, my eyes and my soul were encompassed by an unforgettable scene. In the north reposed the deep, wide valley and all its lakes, over which morning had spread its veil of mist. In the south were the Swiss Alps, their peaks covered with eternal snow. The dazzling snow was traversed by wonderful, shimmering pink streaks; I felt as if I were seeing angels' thoughts caressing the virginal earth. My own eye wept with delight into the eye of Switzerland.

A few years later I climbed Vesuvius. Dawn still reigned around us as we sat beside the crater. Fire was cascading from its triple mouth; fearful crashes raged around it; the whole mountain was smoking. [...] The neighbouring group of mountains wore a strange blue shroud, as if a fire were fuming in their entrails. I shivered like someone who anticipates a future pregnant with misfortune.

Now I was standing on Sinai. A fierce gale was blowing. Jagged masses of granite loomed around me, white clouds lying between their precipitous peaks with the Whitsun morning sun shining down on them. [...] Here I did not experience the delight inspired by the Rigi, nor the strange thrill of Vesuvius; here I felt constrained to pray with fervour, as if God were closer here than anywhere else on earth. His sublimity, his awe-inspiring majesty, his love, his mercy, all combined in one single, glorious sight: such did Sinai appear to me. Like a royal throne set up by God for himself on earth, immutable since the day of creation and built by the same hand that created the pulsating ocean and arched the eternal heavens: such is Sinai. It stands there like a holy fortress, remote from the forums of the world, remote from human habitations, alone between the desert and the sea and towering upward to the clouds. [...] Had I ever dreamt in childhood of some time in the future, holy above all others and promoted from the workaday to the realm of transfiguration, I must have dreamt of this Whitsun time on the summit of Sinai.[1]

Tischendorf got to St Catherine's monastery just before Whitsun. He had scarcely settled in – he had been assigned *a spacious chamber furnished all round with a divan and colourful carpets as a drawing-room, together with a bedroom and a study* – when he heard the mountain's call. *My windows, which looked out over the monastery, afforded a view of Horeb; there it stood before me in the stark nakedness of its grey rock, rugged and forbidding. But a few isolated crucifixes looked down from the heights; nothing was so rugged or daunting as to blunt the hermits' pious enthusiasm.*[2]

So Tischendorf set off on Whit Sunday. He took the same route that I had toiled up. After his trek through the desert, he must have been so fit that the climb made little impression on him. It is, in fact, hard work. Even in the first third, the steep face visible from the monastery, I encountered, coming the other way with a huge rucksack, a solitary young American who was almost out on his feet. He said he had spent hours yesterday climbing the mountain by way of the track and then 'froze his ass off in spite of three blankets'. Even though the view from the summit was 'awesome', he advised me to turn back because the route he had just descended was 'very long and very tough'.

Although I really did begin to wonder whether there was any point in going on, I was loath to be shamed by Moses and his successor, Tischendorf. What is more, at several points in the climb the mountain holds out the illusory hope that the summit is already quite close, only to reveal that the ridge you hoped was the last is the prelude to yet another succession of seemingly interminable steps – and even then you're probably far from the top. However, there are several places on the way where you can rest. You don't really have to climb, either; the route isn't a challenge for genuine mountaineers, just incredibly tiring. After the first third you come to a small chapel dedicated to the Virgin Mary. It is locked and looks a bit dilapidated, but at least you can take a breather there and enjoy your first extensive view of your surroundings. It is still as steep a climb from there on, but you aren't as hemmed in as you are in the gorge that forms the first third of the climb. Your view of the rugged mountainscape becomes more exciting with every step. The price you pay is that there are no more crags to hide the sun, so it becomes quite hot even in winter. In summer the climb must be murderous.

Tischendorf describes this part of the climb as follows: *We soon began to ascend steeply. The route leads upwards between two slopes that fall away into a ravine, passing over numerous rocks that display the remains of hewn steps said to date from the time of Helena* [Constantine's mother, J.G]. *Shrubs, grasses and flowers grow only sparsely. Almost a thousand feet above the monastery we rested beside the limpid spring of St Sangarius. Shortly afterwards, when we had passed two small chapels, I was surprised to see that the route above and ahead of me was spanned by a stone arch with a crucifix, and immediately afterwards by a second, to which we climbed between abruptly projecting rocks.*[3]

I saw what Tischendorf describes when I reached the next ridge. Almost as if this were a village, the monks have installed a passageway that really does resemble a conventional flight of steps. The village impression is reinforced by a masonry gate with an imposing arch at the end of the stairway. This conveys the impression that beyond the gate stands a big house or possibly a church. In fact, this gate used in ancient times to mark the beginning of the mountain's sacred precinct proper. People could climb as far as the gateway, but if they wanted to pass through it they had to prove that their souls were pure. A monk refused them admittance until they had confessed their sins. It paid to undergo this procedure, however, because not far above and beyond the confessional gate the weary traveller came to the loveliest part of Mount Sinai. Visible from afar is the tip of a cypress tree, and the path suddenly debouches into a valley in which cypresses and olive trees grow and a spring yields water at certain times of the year. This place was a refuge favoured by Christian hermits, for it was in this valley that, according to biblical legend, Moses left behind the 40 oldest and wisest members of the tribes of Israel, because the final ascent to God was reserved for him alone. Tischendorf, too, was impressed:

My thoughts were immersed in those early times when so many hermits, fervently dedicating themselves to the Lord, lived and died on this mountain. We were now standing in the oasis of Horeb, which, amid the grey, granite rocks, deploys a cheerful wreath of greenery as if to compensate for their solemn appearance. In its midst, near a basin of cool spring water, stands a solitary cypress. What more agreeable image can be conceived of than this cypress, with its dark, evergreen foliage, its lofty, unbowed crown, its foot planted on Horeb, and its gaze fixed on the summit of Sinai? It stands there like a latter-day prophetic messenger entrusted with the promise of a holy, happy future. Nearby stands

The jagged peaks of southern Sinai, which stretch away to the Red Sea, make crossing the peninsula a very arduous undertaking.

the abandoned chapel of the prophet Elijah, who once dwelt there when he fled from the wrath of Ahab and Jezebel. "Go forth," he was told by the angel of God; "Go forth and stand upon the mount before the Lord." And behold, the Lord passed by, and a great and strong wind rent the mountains and brake in pieces the rocks before the Lord.' Yes, here the Lord passed by: thus did my soul cry out in this consecrated spot; these fractured mountains, these broken rocks, still bear witness, even today, to the footsteps of the Lord.[4]

However, the dramatic mood that sets in when you prepare to make an ascent in the footsteps of Moses and Elijah, personally and in a seemingly exclusive manner, turns to bitter disappointment as soon as you reach the next intermediate summit. Your solitary climb has culminated in a sort of fairground. Before the start of the last 700 steps to the summit proper, your route is met by the camel track along which tourists teeter on the backs of dromedaries.

Goodbye to solitude. Beyond a miniature shanty town, people are streaming up the final 700 steps, part of the way in single file. Although the summit is correspondingly crowded and the mixture of pilgrims and esoteric weirdos who have transformed each hollow into a temporary sleeping place is not conducive to a mood of reverence, most new arrivals fall silent the first time they survey their surroundings from up there. If he was ever here, Moses must have felt intensely depressed by the sight that met his eye: an endless succession of mountains. Particularly in the east, where the Promised Land was reputed to be awaiting the Israelites, one precipitous ridge rubs shoulders with the next. There seems to be no way through for a band of fugitives, not even one assisted by the pillars of cloud and fire God sent to guide them. It is unsurprising, therefore, that in view of the debacle into which Yahweh had led them, the tribes went back to their old gods and swiftly erected a golden calf of hope. The *wadi* that leads to Mount Sinai is indeed a historical cul-de-sac.

So if Moses really did lead the tribes of Israel to this mountain, they must, in order to have had any chance at all of proceeding eastwards, have first withdrawn a few days' march to the north, to the Pharain Oasis. Only there does a valley open up to the east – along which a modern road runs beside the Gulf of Aqaba up to Nuweiba. From there it would doubtless have been possible, even in the 2nd century BC, to reach modern Eilat. If God was merciful to the Israelites, the Jordan, which is now dried up between the Dead Sea and the Gulf, would still have contained some water that would have supplied them with at least a little to drink on their trek across the desert and past today's Dead Sea. Whether or not this band of refugees would have had the strength, on encountering the first fortified city east of the Dead Sea after 40 years of traversing deserts and mountains, to demolish its walls with their trumpets – who knows? The tribes of Judaea and Israel must have been profoundly impressed by their forefathers' heroic deeds.

The Discovery
The secret in the basket

Constantin Tischendorf spent a week as a guest of St Catherine's Monastery in May 1844. The prior of the monastery had assigned him a constant companion in the person of a young man who spoke Italian and French as well as Greek, and thus spared Tischendorf the embarrassment of having to communicate with the monks in fractured Greek. The youth made a good initial impression but was somewhat mentally retarded, which was why the monks treated him as a factotum. He guided Tischendorf all round the desert fortress and enthusiastically showed him the ancient chapels – there are 22 small chapels within that confined space – and the celebrated monastery church. Tischendorf's relations with the monks themselves remained tense. Although, on the way back from the summit, he had encountered almost all the brothers at their Whitsun celebrations in a cave on the mountainside and had been treated to a glass of wine with them, he did not feel at home in the monastery. Until the last, he felt himself being eyed with suspicion, and he remained convinced that the monks would sooner hide their treasures from him than initiate him into the monastery's secrets. What caused a real stir was an allegedly precious evangeliary whose existence he had caught wind of, but which was withheld from him on a series of different pretexts. Sometimes it couldn't be found, sometimes the prior was working on it, and suddenly it was in Cairo, no longer in the monastery at all. Tischendorf lost his temper at this and became positively abusive. He was simply being lied to, he complained to the superior, of whose duplicity he had anyway been convinced at first sight. The man hailed from Crete, he discovered, so he noted with relish in his memoirs that St Paul himself had found on his missionary journeys that *The Cretians are always liars.*

A page from the Codex Sinaiticus from Leipzig University Library.

The great exception among the monks from Tischendorf's point of view was the librarian, Kyrillos. This middle-aged monk came from the big monastic community of Mount Athos in northern Greece and had, Tischendorf believed, been exiled to Sinai. The only monk at St Catherine's who could read ancient Greek, he was an amiable intellectual who took the trouble to introduce Tischendorf to the library's treasures and allowed him to take interesting manuscripts to his room in order to study them at leisure. When Tischendorf arrived at the monastery, Kyrillos was engaged in cataloguing the library's contents. In addition to printed works, there were several hundred manuscripts in ancient Greek, Arabic and Russian, of which *some of the Syrian and Arabic are very old and merit closer examination,* Tischendorf noted. *However,* he reported to his brother, *it is distressing to see precious old uncial manuscripts, some in the form of loose leaves and some bound, lying around and abandoned to destruction thanks to the ignorance and carelessness of the monastery's inhabitants.*[1]

It was not until shortly before his departure that Tischendorf, amid the very disarray he so strongly deplored, made the discovery that changed his life and transformed a palaeographer known only in professional circles into a star who soon attracted the same admiration as Heinrich Schliemann, the excavator of Troy, or Howard Carter, who was to discover the tomb of Tutankhamun early in the 20th century. According to Tischendorf's own account, he was chatting with Kyrillos in the library, when he began, quite casually, to rummage in a basket containing some old sheets of parchment which Kyrillos had probably discarded because he did not know what manuscript they belonged to. While rummaging in the basket, Tischendorf was struck by the majuscule letters on a big sheet of parchment, neatly arrayed in four columns and written in ancient uncial script. The text, he instantly recognized, consisted of passages from the Old Testament. Feverishly, he went on rummaging, and more and more of these fantastic pages came to light. In high excitement, Tischendorf found 43 leaves lying immediately on top of each other, and by the time he had searched and sorted out every last scrap of parchment in the basket there were 129 leaves *in toto,* each filled with four columns of uncial script and all forming parts of a Greek manuscript of the Old Testament. Having in recent years combed every European library for

This was where books used for Mass were kept in St
Catherine's Monastery during the 19th century.

ancient biblical manuscripts, Tischendorf knew at a glance what was
really old or only apparently so, and these sheets, he saw with mounting excitement, were truly ancient. The type of script alone suggested
that they must date from the 4th century. Tischendorf had only once
set eyes on a manuscript as old, and that was the Codex Vaticanus,
which was guarded in Rome as the apple of the Pope's eye.

Tischendorf naturally wanted to take the whole find with him right
away, but his excitement betrayed him. Even good-natured Kyrillos
smelt a rat, it seems, because he allowed the excited German to take
only one batch – the first 43 sheets he had removed from the basket
– to his room with him. There, after close study, he realized that he
had struck archaeological oil. The sheets belonged to the oldest biblical manuscript he had ever seen, so he was dominated by a single
thought: he had to have them.

Tischendorf's discovery of these 129 leaves initiated a still-continuing dispute over the legitimate ownership of the Codex Sinaiticus, the oldest extant biblical manuscript in the world. He initially made a big secret of his find. Having managed to appropriate the first 43 sheets he had removed from the basket for closer study, he took them back to Europe with him. There he copied out the pages, had some type specially cast, and published the whole batch as the Codex Friderico-Augustanus in honour of his patron, King Friedrich August II of Saxony. He carefully avoided giving any indication of the source of his sensational find, however, because he was hoping for more and was fearful of attracting competitors to the site of the discovery.

He did not publish his own version of the find, *Die Sinaibibel – Ihre Entdeckung, Herausgabe und Erwerbung* [The Sinai Bible – Its Discovery, Publication and Acquisition] until 1871, or three years before his relatively early death: *On shelves around the walls in the room that enjoyed the description library were printed and handwritten books. I looked through them one by one. In the middle of the library, however, there was also a large basket containing the remains of damaged manuscripts. When I proceeded to examine this, Kyrillos the librarian remarked that its contents had twice been thrown into the fire. This, therefore, was the third filling, which to all appearances was destined for the same end. I could not fail to be astonished when I removed a number of very large parchment sheets of Greek script whose palaeographic appearance led me to conclude that they were of the greatest antiquity. I had not only seen the oldest Greek manuscripts owned by European libraries but studied them for the purpose of a new Greek palaeography and copied some of them, including the Vatican Bible, with my own hand.* [Tischendorf is mistaken here. At the time of his first discovery he had been permitted only one brief examination of the Codex Vaticanus, J.G.] *Thus, no eye could have been more familiar with old Greek forms of writing. But I had seen nothing that could be regarded as older than the Sinai sheets. Their contents, which proved to be from the Old Testament, were historical and prophetic books, and the sheets numbered 129. The basket's destiny rendered it possible for the smaller, loose batch of leaves, 43 of them, to be surrendered to me at my request. Later, when I endeavoured to acquire the rest, difficulties were raised by the Superior, even though he betrayed no personal knowledge of the matter. I then made an accurate list of the contents of the remaining 86 sheets. They comprised the books of Tobias and Judith, the first and fourth books of the Maccabees, the prophet Isaiah, 6 sheets of Jeremiah, and 9 minor prophets. I also made a verbatim copy of a whole sheet bearing the last three columns of Isaiah and the first of Jeremiah. However, I urgently advised Kyrillos the librarian, who had done me many favours during my sojourn in Sinai, to guard those precious sheets well – and, I added, anything else of the kind that might come to light. For the remains of an ancient volume beside the remaining sheets demonstrated that a comprehensive biblical manuscript had existed here. At the same time, I made no secret to Kyrillos of my intention to pay Sinai another visit; I also intimated to him that I would seek to interest the imperial Russian government in the matter.*[2]

There are two crucial points in this description. For one thing, Tischendorf states that the contents of the basket from which he fished out the oldest known pages of the Bible were destined to be thrown into the fire, so he claimed to be the saviour of that irreplaceable treasure. From this there follows his second assertion: that the fate of the basket's contents made it possible for the smaller part of the find to be surrendered to him at his request. The monks of St Margaret's have fiercely disputed both these allegations for decades. When Father Justin showed me his library 165 years later, in January 2009, he described to me how parchment manuscripts used to be kept at the monastery in the old days. He said it had been quite customary for sheets of parchment to be kept in baskets of the kind Tischendorf had come across, not only in the East but in Europe as well. 'There's a picture in the Vatican that shows the Pope being handed an ancient manuscript from a basket,' Father Justin told me. Parchment sheets had been stored in such baskets for centuries, so the one Tischendorf came across was not a waste-paper basket at all but the normal repository for ancient parchment manuscripts. According to Father Justin's research, the last original parchment basket in St Margaret's had been taken away to London by a visiting Englishwoman at the end of the 19th century. More important, he said, it was positively ridiculous to claim that the sheets would have been burnt. Parchment is scraped hide, and hide burns badly. Besides, parchment was a very valuable material. Unlike papyrus, its predecessor as a writing material, it was almost imperishable and thus, as Tischendorf must have known from personal experience, reused rather than destroyed. If an ancient text became redundant it was scraped off and the parchment written on afresh. The whole thing was then called a palimpsest, and Tischendorf himself had won fame for deciphering one such. Parchment had remained in use for binding books even when it was superseded by paper. Father Justin said that no modern expert gave credence to Tischendorf's claim that he had saved the Sinai Bible sheets from the flames in the nick of time.

For that reason, Justin went on, it was still unclear how Tischendorf had come into possession of the 43 sheets. There was no documentary evidence to show that those sheets, which Leipzig University Library now preserves in its safe, were ever presented to him. Tischendorf's own account suggests that Kyrillos the librarian had relinquished them to him unofficially, so to speak, but he got cold feet when Tischendorf wanted the remaining 86 sheets as well and consulted the father superior. As Tischendorf himself says, although the latter had no precise knowledge of what was really involved, he objected to relinquishing the sheets to an interloper from the West.

But Tischendorf was firmly resolved from the first to bring the sheets to Europe. On the day he met with resistance from the father superior, the man with the 'duplicitous' expression, he began to debate how to get his hands on the sheets just the same. He then, at the end of his life, revealed that he at once thought of a potential source of help. He would endeavour, he told Kyrillos, to 'interest' the imperial Russian court.

By the time Tischendorf was received by the imperial Russian ambassador in Constantinople a few weeks later, he was already toying with the idea of requesting his help in acquiring the sheets still at the monastery, but at the last moment he shrank from revealing his secret. His brother was the only person he confided in. Immediately after returning to Cairo in June 1844, he listed the results of his expedition: *Listen now to the substantial products of my research. I have come into possession of 43 parchment sheets of the O.T. in Greek, which are the very oldest of any such possessed by Europe. I believe them to date from the middle of the 4th century. That is a quite inestimable treasure, which, apart from its incomparable antiquity, abounds in remarkable features. I also possess 24 sheets of palimpsests in Arabic script from the 12th century and one in Greek from the 8th to 9th; furthermore, 4 similar palimpsest sheets and, finally, in addition to other less important items, 4 mutilated sheets of a Greek manuscript of the N.T. from 7–800. These things will cause a great stir.*[3]

Homecoming

In a subsequent letter posted to his brother from Constantinople in September 1844, Tischendorf was already envisaging what awaited him back home. *When you wrote to me, you had yet to receive the news of my principal conquest in the way of manuscripts; you will have considered me fortunate when you read it. I feel delighted whenever I think of it; or was it a mere bagatelle to salvage this manuscript, which may well be the very oldest of all the parchment documents in Europe, and bring it back to dear Saxony and enduring fame? My travels in the East have thus been blessed, and have surpassed the expectations of friend and foe alike. I still do not know what I shall do with my manuscripts; I considered handing them all over to the government and expecting, in return, a higher than usual professorial salary, possibly as much as 800 th, but I think I could claim something else for them. I've no wish to rack my brains prematurely.*[4]

Although Tischendorf had no wish to rack his brains for the moment, he was firmly resolved to use his discovery to secure his financial position. He had had a hard time fending for himself since his parents' death, and now he wanted a reward for his exertions. When he wrote the above lines he had still to become a professor, let alone a highly-paid one. He was not mistaken, though, because the court at Dresden later proved generous. Tischendorf leapfrogged every university committee and was appointed to an extraordinary chair of philosophy. The post carried no tutorial obligations. In any case, he was initially engaged in publishing his great find as the Codex Friderico-Augustanus, not least in order to legitimize his extraordinary appointment.

Tischendorf returned to Saxony in December 1844, but instead of hurrying to his fiancée Angelika Zehme, he went to Lengenfeld to see his brother Julius, who was by way of being head of the family now that their parents were dead. He spent the Christmas holidays in his brother's company. Even before leaving Constantinople he had written to Julius to tell him that he proposed to deliver the Christmas sermon at Lengenfeld and to ask him to inform the priest in charge. The sermon became a public relations exercise on his own behalf. Tischendorf described his expedition to the origins of Christianity, and in one passage touched on the differences between Orthodoxy and his beloved Lutheran Church: *Our Church, the Evangelical Church, possesses a glorious treasure which is sadly not known and appreciated by all; this is our hymn-singing, the singing of our fine hymns, the like of which no nation save the German has produced. Luther, who was most concerned to encourage hymn-singing, thoroughly understood that. This part of our church services provides us with far more than a mere substitute for the ostentatious customs of other denominations.*[5]

In January 1845, almost five years after leaving Leipzig, he at long last returned to the city by way of the newly-built railway line. From there he set off for Städteln, but not without previously writing to Angelika to chide her for having complained about his long absence. Before they married in September the same year, he sent her a letter making it clear, yet again, that his career took precedence over all else: *The fact that I see you in Städteln less often than you wish and than I myself would like is rooted in the serious nature of my life, as I told you long ago. It is a very good thing that you cannot estrange me therefrom. You know I have always intimated to you that my life is oriented thus.*[6]

In view of her fiancé's unambiguous priorities, Angelika Zehme must have had grave doubts about the wisdom of marrying him, for Tischendorf more than once complained of her vacillation. Nevertheless, having grown up in the home of a conservative, pietistic clergyman, Angelika eventually went her predestined way: she married Professor Constantin Tischendorf, a court favourite whose chest was already adorned with several orders, and who guaranteed her a comfortable future. Besides, she had been brought up in the faith in such a way that her views would largely have coincided with his.

It turned out to be a marriage of the kind that is mapped out in advance: Constantin travelled the world while Angelika looked after the household and their ever more numerous brood of children.

Although he was seldom in Leipzig, he indulged in no escapades. Even later on, at the zenith of his fame, he was never unfaithful to her and, notwithstanding many exotic temptations, remained true to his convictions. A patriarch who never questioned his own dominant role, he regarded Angelika as a helpmate whose support he took for granted but with whom he retained an intimate relationship.

For the first few years after his return from Sinai, he joined her in establishing a middle-class existence in Leipzig, where they found a house appropriate to his professorial status. He closely devoted himself to his studies but travelled from time to time, *inter alia* to London, where he spent some months working at the British Museum. He was introduced to people of the highest rank, not only at the court of Saxony but at that of King Friedrich Wilhelm IV of Prussia in Berlin. There he made the acquaintance of Friedrich Wilhelm von Schelling, the well-known philosopher, and of the polymath Alexander von Humboldt, who is said to have commented very favourably on his scholarship. But one question continued to haunt Tischendorf throughout these years: What about the 86 sheets of parchment still at St Catherine's? He was obsessed with the fear that some competitor – particularly one of the British archaeologists who roamed the Near East in ever-increasing numbers – might steal a march on him. Shortly after he returned, having put his finances in order and bequeathed all his acquisitions to Leipzig University Library in return for a goodly sum, he wrote to his friend in Cairo, Pruner Bey, the viceroy's personal physician, to enlist his support. He requested that Pruner Bey ask the monks to sell the sheets for a 'substantial sum', which he proposed to place at his disposal. But Pruner Bey declined. 'I know from a friend who has just returned from the Sinai monastery,' he wrote back, 'that since your departure it has been common knowledge at the monastery that the monks possess a treasure. The more you offer, the less inclined they will be to relinquish the manuscript.'[7]

Tischendorf accepted this for the moment. He worked on a new edition of his Greek Bible and reinforced his status, but he never considered giving up. Late in 1850, after almost five years, he wrote the court a long memorandum in which he broached the idea of another trip to the East. He described all that could still be found in the way of aids to critical textual research into the New Testament and why he was especially predestined to undertake this task. To prevent his request from being shelved, he impressed upon the minister of education (who was also responsible for the university) that the danger that he – and Saxony – would be forestalled by English scholars was growing year by year. Nothing stirred at court, however; his patrons' interest seemed to have waned. Tischendorf thereupon played his greatest trump card: he revealed his secret to von Beust, the current minister of education. He told him precisely where he had found the celebrated parchment sheets and, more importantly, that there were many more of them. *Thereafter he readily granted me the support I needed to make the journey,*[8] Tischendorf noted laconically. If he couldn't acquire the sheets, he wanted at least to copy them all and render them accessible to biblical scholarship.

Disappointment

Tischendorf set off for Egypt in January 1853, only to meet with absolute disaster. Everything went more quickly this time, admittedly, and technological progress made itself felt. The ship took only a week to get from Trieste to Alexandria, whence a steamer conveyed him up the Nile to Cairo. Only those who know how much Tischendorf hated sea travel can gauge how obsessed he was with his find in the Sinai monastery. *He who wishes to learn to pray,* he wrote to Angelika, *must go to sea. I am sending you a song that emerged from my soul at the end of our stormy voyage.* Tischendorf the Protestant literally kept his head above water by praying and singing.

In Cairo he met many of his old acquaintances and immediately organized a new expedition to the monastery in Sinai, where he had not been forgotten either. To his great delight, Kyrillos the librarian was still there and in his wonted place. The situation was maddening, however. Kyrillos had forgotten where the 86 parchment sheets were – indeed, he even claimed not to remember them at all. Becoming thoroughly suspicious, Tischendorf did not believe a word of this. He now felt convinced that he really had come too late. The sheets, his precious parchment pages of the Old Testament, had simply disappeared. Search as he might, he found only one little clue. *In a much more recent Greek codex containing hagiographies, which I was leafing through in search of apocryphal Acts, I found, like a bookmark, a small sheet, a hand's-breadth across, which had unmistakably belonged to the same old biblical manuscript. It bore a few verses from the 24th chapter of Genesis. This meant that I was holding in my hands fresh evidence that a complete manuscript of the Old Testament might originally have been there,*[9] Tischendorf noted in his late work. The wily monks must have sold the sheets, of that the Saxon scholar was firmly convinced – probably, he surmised, to a well-heeled Englishman. He felt betrayed.

Outwardly, however, he made the best of a bad job and later claimed that his trip had been a complete success. *My scientific results are outstanding,* he wrote to Angelika. *They have fully covered my travelling expenses.* He had also been mindful of his children, for whom he collected some particularly fine shells from the Red Sea. Secretly disappointed, he returned home only three months later.

Back in Leipzig, Tischendorf promptly threw himself into his work with characteristic pertinacity. The sheets in Sinai had long since become his ruling obsession. The precious relics had to be somewhere, and he expected some rival to brandish them under his nose at any moment. But nothing happened. He then tried to coax the secret possessors of the Sinai sheets out of their shell. In the first volume of a Christian document compendium which he had just started, intending it to include all the documents that had been handed down from the early centuries of Christianity, he quoted such extensive passages from the 86 sheets he had copied at the monastery that those in the know would be bound to realize that he knew of their existence. *On the one hand,* he noted later, *I meant to persuade the fortunate second finder, who appeared to have carried off the precious sheets, not to withhold them from the world of scholarship any longer; on the other, I wanted to claim the honour of their discovery for myself.* But absolutely nothing happened; no competitor broke cover, no sensational publication appeared. *My thoughts had lagged far behind the ways of Providence,*[10] he wrote.

Tischendorf's hopes revived. He might not be too late after all, but he wanted to be really well prepared before setting off for Sinai a third time. He proposed to turn up at the monastery no longer as a poor Saxon scholar and petitioner, but as an envoy of the supreme Orthodox authority, the Tsar of Russia. By now well acquainted with courtly customs, he proceeded to explore the terrain, but his timing could not have been worse.

Envoy of the Tsar

Tischendorf's return to Leipzig from his second trip coincided with the preliminary skirmishes of the Crimean War. Russian troops occupied Wallachia and Moldavia, principalities that nominally still belonged to the Ottoman Empire. Tischendorf must have been pleased by the Tsar's immediate pretext for wresting control over the Dardanelles and the Bosphorus from the weakened Ottoman Empire. This was a dispute over the Church of the Holy Sepulchre in Jerusalem. In the middle of the 19th century the 'Holy Land', too, still belonged to the Ottomans, so the Sultan was the supreme guardian of the holy places in both Mecca and Jerusalem. At this time, however, Christians were not fighting Muslims in Jerusalem; they were fighting among themselves. Greek Orthodox and other Eastern churches such as the Armenian, Syrian and Coptic were disputing control of and access to the Church of the Holy Sepulchre with the Roman Catholics. The Tsar of Russia, Nicholas I, regarded himself as the supreme protector of Orthodoxy and demanded that the Sultan in Constantinople yield control over the Christian shrines in Jerusalem to himself. The Sultan, who was uninterested in the squabble over the Church of the Holy Sepulchre, was at first inclined to accommodate the Tsar, but two things stood in the way of this. In the first place, France was an Ottoman ally and firmly opposed to such a move. Napoleon III posed as protector of the Catholics and refused to give ground to the Tsar. Secondly, the Tsar increased his demands every time the Sultan gave way, so the Ottoman court was left with no alternative but to refuse. This provided the protector of Orthodoxy with his pretext for war.

Tsar Nicholas I was so preoccupied with the war that he would hardly have been responsive to talk of an ancient biblical manuscript. Two years later, in 1855, he died quite suddenly and his son succeeded him as Alexander II. Alexander was of a different calibre from his father. Quickly realizing that the war was a mistake that had proved to be a real setback to Russia's European ambitions, he was eager to end it as soon as possible. The peace treaty was signed a year after he came to the throne. Alexander was the last Russian Tsar to make strenuous political efforts to modernize his huge and structurally medieval empire. He became a reformer who, in 1881, was tragically murdered by an assassin belonging to the secret lodge of the progressive *Narodnaya Volya* (Friends of the People). In consequence of the lost Crimean War, however, he did initiate an army reform, endeavoured to restructure the bureaucracy more effectively, and in 1861 – his greatest achievement – abolished serfdom.

Alexander II was not given to religious enthusiasm, but a court consists of more than the monarch. Tischendorf slowly worked his way towards the Tsarist court, and he evidently knew whom to put his money on. He compiled an extensive file in which, in addition to Sinai, much emphasis was laid on the monastic republic of Mount Athos in the northern Aegean, because he knew that Abraham von Norov, the Russian minister of education, had a soft spot for it. He then approached the imperial ambassador in Dresden, Baron Schröder, and requested him to forward his memorandum to Norov. The latter, who fell for it at once, even came to Dresden in person to meet Tischendorf and discuss a joint visit to the monasteries on Mount Athos.

But there were difficulties. The Russian Church was naturally reluctant to prejudice its own interests. If at all, it wanted to send a delegation to its Orthodox brothers in the East. One of its senior priests, Archimandrite Porfiry Uspensky, later bishop of Kiev, had himself visited St Catherine's monastery in Sinai and could thus see no reason why Russia should finance a German Protestant's expedition to the Egyptian desert. What Tischendorf did not know, and what the monks in Sinai had concealed from him during his second stay at the monastery, was that Uspensky had twice been to St Catherine's between Tischendorf's first and second visits in 1844 and 1853, and that he had personally examined the 86 sheets of ancient manuscript Tischendorf so sorely missed. What was more, Uspensky had actually seen far more of them, but, just like Tischendorf, had made no mention of this when reporting on his travels. However, Tischendorf had an unexpected stroke of luck. Uspensky was no manuscript expert, had received far less academic training than Tischendorf, and did not belong to the exclusive inner circle of European palaeographers, so he was unacquainted with Tischendorf's publication of the Codex Friderico-Augustanus – indeed, just like the monks of the monastery, he had failed to detect how old the manuscript was and, consequently, how valuable. Critical textual research was as rare in Russia's Orthodox Church as it was among the Sinaite monks, as Uspensky would amply demonstrate in a subsequent dispute with Tischendorf.

Just to complete Tischendorf's misfortunes, not only was he opposed by the Church, but his patron Norov lost his ministerial job. His successor, Minister von Kovalevsky, was totally uninterested in the project at first and, when Tischendorf wrote from Leipzig pressing for a decision, merely informed him that his budget had no money to spare for a scheme like his. Tischendorf seemed to have reached the end of the road once more, but he did have one last trump card in his hand. The name of the trump card was Theodor von Grimm, a Saxon scholar and former tutor to the Tsar's brother, Grand Duke Constantine, who was currently back in St Petersburg as tutor to the crown prince. Tischendorf proceeded to employ Theodor von Grimm as his secret weapon in Russia.

Their first target was Grand Duke Constantine. Alexander was a down-to-earth monarch, whereas his brother had time and leisure enough to perpetuate the family's traditional religious fervour. Constantine, who already took a great personal interest in Christianity's holy places in the East, allowed Grimm to infect him with enthusiasm for Tischendorf's project. He quickly realized what a propaganda coup it would be for the royal house if parts of the world's oldest Bible came to St Petersburg, thereby legitimizing the role of the Tsars as guardians of Orthodoxy. He backed the scheme, therefore, but Tischendorf owed his ultimate success to a female compatriot from Hessen. Tsar Alexander was married, albeit unhappily, to a German princess, Maria von Hessen-Darmstadt, and the Tsarina was even more enthusiastic about Tischendorf's project than Constantine. In the summer of 1858 the court left St Petersburg for several weeks and went to Moscow. Just before the empress's departure, Tischendorf's agent, Theodor von Grimm, handed her a paper which ex-Minister Norov had drafted as a basis for the Tsar's decision.

We have a rough idea of how hard the empress must have badgered her long-suffering husband into sanctioning her compatriot's expedition, because, for whatever reasons, he gave his approval the next day. Tischendorf got all he wanted: money in the form of gold at his free disposal and the assurance that he could make use of the whole of the Russian diplomatic corps within the Ottoman Empire. Most important of all, he could present himself in Sinai as an envoy of the Tsar, and he was entitled to hope that the monks would cooperate with someone in the Tsar's service.

Tischendorf learnt of Alexander II's favourable decision in September 1858. At the end of November, acting on behalf of the Tsar, Prince Volkonsky gave him money 'in Russian gold' intended to cover not only his travelling expenses but also any potential acquisitions. *I neither had to make out a receipt of any kind, nor did I receive any word of instruction or obligation, so thoroughly did imperial munificence brand the venture a matter of high-minded trust,* Tischendorf boasted later.[11]

I go in the name of the Lord

Once again, Tischendorf embarked for Alexandria at Trieste, where he already enjoyed the advantages of travelling in the Tsar's service.

On 10 January 1859, the eve of his departure from Trieste, he quickly wrote his wife a letter: *Incidentally, so far on my journey, no one has considered searching my effects; the mere phrase 'I'm travelling on behalf of His Imperial Russian Majesty' proved omnipotent.* He was also delighted to inform his wife that the directors of Lloyd's had *insisted on placing at my disposal the government tender that will convey me out to the ship tomorrow.*[12]

Provided in this way with gold and protection and travelling as a quasi-diplomat, Tischendorf sailed to Egypt, where, on 16 January, he went ashore for the third time in 16 years.

Alexandria and Cairo were now connected by rail, and on 18 January 1859, his 44th birthday, he pulled into Cairo station after a trip of only six hours, in good spirits and glorious weather. Having lost no time in looking up his old friends in Cairo, Tischendorf hurried on a few days later. Trains now ran to Suez as well, so that was how he began his last trip to the monastery on 23 January. In Suez he had to mount a camel again. The ride across the desert, although shorter than on his previous expeditions, no longer seemed an exciting adventure to the 44-year-old professor; more than anything else, he found it a physical ordeal. The heat and the immense difference between day and nighttime temperatures got him down. *Nevertheless, nothing could rob my heart of the pleasure I felt at my third trip to Sinai in 16 years,* he informed Angelika later.[13]

The Tsar's envoy made as excellent progress in the Sinai monastery as he had in Trieste, Alexandria and Cairo. The monks, who already knew that he was this time travelling on the Tsar's behalf, greeted him accordingly. Only his Russian letter of accreditation was hauled up in a basket through the hole in the wall; he himself was personally welcomed outside the gates by the Oikonomos, the monk responsible for the monastery's domestic management, and conducted to Prior Dionysos, who was ill, by way of a secret passage that ran from the garden and beneath the fortifications. As he wrote to his wife: *The Superior, the head of the monastery, and the other monks treated me like a good spirit sent from above. They spoke of my great achievements for the Church as of things extremely well known to them. Their only wish was that the Lord would again enable me to find what I sought for the Church's benefit. I was thoroughly surprised by such a reception, believe me, but I gladly submitted thereto.*[14]

Tischendorf made every effort to justify his new status. He *quite frankly,* as he put it, informed the monks that he had come, in the Tsar's name and with his gold, to make 'acquisitions' on his behalf; in other words, to purchase those parts of the 4th-century manuscript which he had seen 16 years earlier, together with any other fragments of the ancient Bible that might still exist in the monastery. A letter to his wife put it this way: *I behaved more like a Russian prince than a Saxon professor. I gave presents at every opportunity. My favour and my good offices in St Petersburg were frequently requested.* For all that, he added, *there was no direct, official route to my goal; I had to make private arrangements.*[15]

This allusion in a letter to his wife, dated 15 February 1859, immediately after his return from the monastery to Cairo, leads one to surmise that the ensuing sensation was not quite as adventitious as it appears from the account – the official version, so to speak – presented in the book he wrote shortly before his death.

According to this, he claimed *never to have enquired again about the Biblical fragments I had saved from destruction; I had become convinced since my visit in 1853 that no more of them remained in St Catherine's monastery.*[16] This cannot be right because, after he had hinted at the fragments' existence and no publication or other form of echo had resulted, Tischendorf had come to St Catherine's in the hope that, despite his lack of success in 1853, the sheets might still be hidden in the monastery, and that this time, with the Tsar's support and gold, the fragments might be brought to light once more.

Tischendorf's allusion to 'private arrangements' indicates how he may have attained his objective. The key figure in this respect was the young Oikonomos who had greeted him outside the monastery gates. He came from Athens – no name is ever mentioned – and was, according to Tischendorf, the spiritual foster son of his friend Kyrillos the librarian.

The subsequent course of events is alleged to have been as follows. Having already ordered Bedouin and camels for his return journey on the following Monday (it was now Thursday), Tischendorf joined the Oikonomos on a long walk to the far side of Mount Sinai. They had a frank and lively conversation. Tischendorf had presented the monastery with a copy of his last, 7th edition of the Old and New Testaments in Greek, and the Oikonomos had taken an interest in it. On the way back, just before they reached the monastery, he apparently disclosed to Tischendorf that he, too, was in possession of a Greek Bible. If Tischendorf wished, he could show it to him.

When we returned to the monastery at dusk, the Oikonomos invited me to partake of some refreshments in his cell. As he set them in front of me, he remarked: I also have here a Greek Old Testament. So saying, he went into a corner of his room, brought out a large manuscript wrapped in a red cloth, and deposited it on the table in front of me. Opening the cloth, which was fastened, I saw to my great surprise the splendid uncial script, divided into four columns, of the Codex Friderico-Augustanus.

The leaves were so numerous, they proved at once that they were not restricted to those Old Testament fragments which I had removed from the fateful basket and left behind. A few fleeting glances at them enabled me to discern the beginning and end of the New Testament, with the Epistle of Barnabas, and my surprise became extreme.[17]

According to Tischendorf's account, several more monks suddenly appeared in the cell, Kyrillos among them, and watched him holding the long-sought treasure in his hands, beaming with joy like the Three Kings in the stable.

I asked if I might take the whole cloth and its contents – the leaves were unbound – to my room for closer examination; the good Oikonomos permitted this.

I was beside myself with joy as I hurried into my own cell with them, he reported to his wife not long afterwards. *The first thing I saw was that they contained the whole of the New Testament: it is the only manuscript of its kind in the world! Neither the Codex Vaticanus nor the London Alexandrinus contains the whole NT, and the Sinaite codex is undoubtedly older than either. And now some new surprises. At the end of the book* [i.e. the New Testament, J.G.] *is the complete Epistle of Barnabas, [...] of which a substantial part has until now been accounted lost, in the original Greek. I had tears in my eyes and my heart was moved as never before. When I had recovered, I thought how easily the Shepherd of Hermas might also have been there. I picked up a leaf – some of the leaves are separate – and what did I read? The Shepherd. I then lost my composure altogether, but I felt it in the uttermost depths of my heart: that which had given me no peace at home, much as it also had to do with human endeavour and desire, was the call of the Lord. Although I had always said, I go in the name of the Lord and search for treasures that will bear fruit for his Church, I now knew this to be so and positively took fright at the truth itself. This find is an event. The whole manuscript in its present form is an incomparable treasure for scholarship and the Church.*[18]

And, of course, for Constantin Tischendorf himself. He had worked his way towards it for 16 years, had overcome repeated setbacks, had swallowed disappointments and never given up. He had now attained his goal. It can be inferred from his allusions in the letter to his wife written in the euphoria immediately succeeding his great success that this finale, too, was not quite as fortuitous as he later made out. The monks were certainly not as clueless as the Tsar's envoy would have us believe.

It is probable that, after Tischendorf had identified their manuscript as a valuable relic in June 1844, they proceeded to conduct a search of their own to see if more such manuscript sheets existed. What proves that they discovered them is that, in the years between Tischendorf's first and second visits, Archimandrite Uspensky had laid hands on the whole batch of 347 sheets – the ones that were now relinquished to Tischendorf. Tischendorf learnt that after his first visit the monks had found the 261 sheets which had now been handed him, in addition to the 86 he already knew from 1844, in a second library used for storing manuscripts for liturgical use in the church.

Why did the monks conceal this find from Tischendorf on his second visit in 1853, even though they had previously shown the manuscript to Uspensky? We can only surmise that at least some of the monks must have been toying, early on, with the idea of using the manuscript as a bargaining counter *vis-à-vis* the Tsarist court. When Tischendorf turned up as an envoy of the Tsar, he was of more interest to them than he had been as a private hunter of lost manuscripts. The Oikonomos declined to sell him the manuscript, however. By his own account, Tischendorf offered to acquire it in return for gold and a substantial donation to the monastery the morning after the find, since it was *useless* in the monastery itself.

But the Oikonomos refused – an act for which Tischendorf himself had *great understanding*. Instead, he put forward another suggestion: the monastery should officially donate the Codex Sinaiticus to the Tsar. This suggestion had obvious merits because the monks of Sinai were hoping for the Tsar's political protection as well as money. Meanwhile, however, Tischendorf wanted to start as soon as possible on carefully copying all the sheets in order to be able to publish a scholarly edition. He was anxious to take the manuscript back to Cairo, where he would be able to work on it more effectively, but for that he needed the approval of the elders of the Sinaite Church, currently assembled in Cairo to elect a successor to Archbishop Constantios, who had died at the age of 100 only a few days earlier.

Tischendorf hurried to Cairo as fast as he could. There, having received the permission he sought, he employed a sheikh of the Sinai nomads to go and fetch the precious manuscript. He whetted the sheikh's appetite for speed by reaching into his sack of gold once more, and the man was back in Cairo after an incredible ten days. *On 24 February 1859, a monk brought me the precious package by dromedary post. We then agreed at the Russian consulate-general that I should take away individual batches of eight sheets apiece for copying, and I made an immediate start.*[19]

In the Tsar's Service

Art theft or conservation?

In the middle of the old quarter of Greifswald, Germany's eastern-most Hanseatic city, stands a building of colossal proportions. This is the cathedral, a Gothic relic of medieval brick so monumental it looks as if it would easily accommodate the entire population of Greifswald. Nearly 100 metres high, the tower projects far above the city's skyline and its viewing platform looks out over the Baltic, western Pomerania, and the islands of Rügen and Usedom. Surrounding the cathedral is the wonderfully restored old quarter, which contains two more churches that now look rather oversized as well. But Greifswald used to be a powerful Hanseatic city. The university, one of the first in Germany, was founded in the cathedral back in 1456, and the cathedral has been a stronghold of Protestantism ever since the Reformation. A plaque on the south wall pays tribute to King Gustavus Adolphus of Sweden, protector of the Protestant faith, whose intervention in the Thirty Years' War in 1630 is said to have preserved Protestantism in the land of Luther.

In the shadow of the cathedral, only a few steps from the main portal, lies Greifswald University's modern theological faculty. Its New Testament specialist, who also preaches in the cathedral from time to time, is Christfried Böttrich. Professor Böttrich is not a Hanseatic Greifswalder. He arrived in the city only a few years ago; before that he worked in Leipzig, among other places, hence his interest in one of his prominent predecessors at Leipzig University, Constantin von Tischendorf. At first out of personal interest but later, too, with scholarly exactitude, he devoted himself to the study of the man he calls 'the most interesting personality at Leipzig University in the second half of the 19th century'. In 1999, in addition to a Tischendorf bibliography, he published a collection of Tischendorf's letters in book form, and in 2005 he published a long article on Tischendorf's role in transferring the Codex Sinaiticus to St Petersburg. In short, Christfried Böttrich is *the* Tischendorf expert in Germany. If anyone knows about the Sinai Codex's convoluted history since 1859, it is he.

The question of how and under what circumstances the codex went first to St Petersburg, which was then the Russian capital, and later to the British Museum in London is of more than historical interest. To this day, the monks of Sinai are convinced that they lost possession of the manuscript under suspicious circumstances, and that their predecessors were, to put it crudely, taken for a ride. 'The codex', the librarian of St Catherine's told me in January 2009, loud and clear, 'belongs back here in the monastery.' Tischendorf does not enjoy a good reputation among the monks of Sinai. Even though they no longer publicly accuse him of theft, they are all, up to and including Archbishop Damianos, convinced that the German scholar played them false. Instead of returning the codex to the monastery after scientifically evaluating it and producing a facsimile edition, Tischendorf and the then Russian government took advantage of the monastery's predicament and coerced those in authority to donate it to Tsar Alexander II of Russia. 'Morally', says Father Justin, 'the codex still belongs to us.'

Professor Christfried Böttrich does not take that view. When I visited him in Greifswald in February 2010, he had almost completed another investigation of the controversial subject. 'The gift was undoubtedly legal', he said, 'and who is now entitled to claim the moral right to this early Christian artefact 'is a difficult question'.

At all events, Tischendorf from the outset had made no secret of his desire to purchase the precious sheets, the earliest written version of the New Testament, or to take them to Europe in some other form. When the monks refused to sell, he had expressed his understanding of their attitude and tried to persuade the head of the monastery that a gift to the Tsar would also be to their advantage.

While he was busy copying the codex with the help of two other Germans, a young English scholar came to the Sinaite monastery in Cairo to see the historical treasure. According to Tischendorf's account, he immediately offered to buy the manuscript from the monks with a view to taking it back to England. The head of the monastery refused, however. Tischendorf later recorded what the monks told him: *'We would rather make Emperor Alexander a gift of the manuscript than sell it for English gold'. I had long been endeavouring to foster that attitude in the monastery. I was glad of this and relied on it subsequently.*[1]

This was the start of the 'donation' project. It became a ten-year tug-of-war whose complications still involve the Sinaite Church, scholars from Leipzig, St Petersburg, Athens, and the United States, and, last but not least, one of the biggest libraries in the world, the British Library. For a donation to the Tsar, Tischendorf needed the approval of all the controlling bodies of the Sinaite brotherhood, and above all that of the archbishop, its spiritual and administrative head. But he was out of luck. Just when the precious packet of 346 double-page parchment sheets had been made accessible to him, His Holiness Constantios, the Sinaites' venerable archbishop, died in far-off Constantinople. Archbishop Constantios was 100 years old at that juncture and had controlled the fortunes of the Sinaite Church since 1805, even at one stage becoming ecumenical patriarch of the whole Orthodox Church. Constantios, whom Tischendorf had met on the way back from his first trip in 1844, was an experienced diplomat thanks to his long service in the capital of the Ottoman Empire, and he must at once have grasped the value of the codex as a bargaining counter for political and financial assistance. His death created a completely different situation, however. The Sinaite brothers had to choose a successor, and Tischendorf could not expect a decision before the new man had been elected and acknowledged by all the relevant ecclesiastical and political authorities.

At first, though, the donation project's prospects did not look bad. The Sinaite brothers agreed on a successor surprisingly quickly and chose a monk named Kyrillos to be their new archbishop. Only a few days after his election, Tischendorf met the new head of the Sinaite Church, who also led him to hope that he would 'give serious consideration' to donating the manuscript to Tsar Alexander II. That the Sinaites considered such a donation to the Russian emperor a serious option at all can be explained by the political situation of the time.

Christian minorities in the Ottoman Empire

The Ottoman Empire was crumbling badly by the middle of the 19th century, but it still controlled vast areas in the Near East, the Balkans, and around the Black Sea. Egypt and the Sinai Peninsula, although kept on a long leash, were as much a part of the Ottoman Empire as Palestine, Cyprus, Crete and Macedonia, or almost everywhere the Sinaite Church was at home. A large percentage of the population in the empire was Christian. The Christians were tolerated by the Muslim sultanate as members of a 'book religion'; they were largely autonomous, administratively speaking, and subject to the jurisdiction of their own church, but they were also second-class citizens to the extent that they could not aspire to senior government posts, had to pay higher taxes, and were excluded from the army. As the empire declined and the European powers' influence in Constantinople grew, however, pressure increased on the Ottoman court to ameliorate the status of Christians in government and put them legally on a par with Muslim subjects.

In these controversies the Tsars played the role of protectors of the Greek Orthodox Church. Although the loss of the Crimean War had perceptibly diminished Russia's influence in Constantinople and simultaneously strengthened that of Britain and France, Russia remained Orthodoxy's big brother. The monastery in Sinai received financial donations from St Petersburg and applied in case of contentious issues to the Tsar's ambassador in Constantinople. For a newly elected archbishop, particularly one compelled to follow in the footsteps of a legendary predecessor, it would doubtless be advantageous to attract the attention and secure the benevolence of the Tsarist court by means of an act such as the donation of a valuable manuscript, which might result in a substantial contribution to the monastery's exchequer. For the Tsar, it was clear from the first, would naturally signify his appreciation of the gift with an appropriate sum in gold roubles.

But Kyrillos, the new archbishop, had an additional reason for getting on the right side of St Petersburg. He did not, like most monks, hail from Greece or a Greek-dominated part of the empire like Cyprus, Crete or Mount Athos, but from the Balkans; more precisely, from the monastery of Fistizios in Wallachia, or modern Romania. An insurrection was then in progress in this corner of the Ottoman Empire, its aim being to render the principality independent. Although fighting the Muslims under the Christian banner, the new masters believed that the Orthodox Church's considerable possessions should be nationalized, so the autonomous Sinaite Church was in danger of losing Fistizios, one of its wealthiest monasteries. It is quite possible that Kyrillos was elected partly because he came from Fistizios, knew the conflict best, and seemed the candidate most likely to preserve the Sinaites' property. For that he needed Russian support, however, and the donation might be a way of securing the requisite assistance.

Tischendorf was bound to have been aware of these circumstances, so he felt confident that he could soon count on a decision in his favour. But unexpected difficulties arose. To be able to officiate in full as archbishop, Kyrillos needed the confirmation of the Sublime Porte, recognition by the ecumenical patriarch in Constantinople, and consecration by the patriarch in Jerusalem, who thus, in practice, had a right of veto over the appointment of the Sinaites' archbishop. But the patriarch in Jerusalem, whose name was also Kyrill, refused to consecrate his namesake as archbishop, and without that consecration Kyrillos had no authority to make the donation.

It is not entirely clear why the patriarch declined to recognize the Sinaites' choice. Perhaps Kyrillos was too pro-Russian for him, or perhaps he really did believe him to be corrupt, as was rumoured, and rejected him on that account. It is also probable that, for reasons hard to reconstruct today, personal antipathy played a part. This was annoying for Tischendorf because the donation now became a distant prospect. But Tischendorf would not have been Tischendorf had he simply looked on idly as his once-in-a-lifetime find threatened to elude him. He knew that his most important patron at the court of St Petersburg, Grand Duke Constantine, the Tsar's brother, had planned a trip to Jerusalem. Tischendorf now received news that the grand duke would arrive in Palestine in a few days' time. He decided to go there himself at once, hoping to enlist his help in changing the patriarch's mind.

In a letter to the grand duke he told of his magnificent discovery, a *treasure for the Christian Church and for scholarship*, and hastened to inform him of his wish to lay this treasure at his feet in Jerusalem. Not the original, which he had vainly tried to purchase, but a meticulous copy of the parchments, which was already complete. Tischendorf wrote that the discovery had become known in Cairo contrary to his wishes, mentioned the English agent who had also tried to buy the codex, and reported that he had already sent information to this effect to St Petersburg, to Education Minister Kovalevsky and His Majesty the Tsar himself. Tischendorf had further written a report for the *Leipziger Zeitung* announcing his triumph. *To my very great pleasure, however,* he informed the grand duke, *I can add that the Sinai monastery authorities have in recent weeks formally consented to the original itself being donated through me to His Imperial Majesty.*[2] He did not mention that the patriarch of Jerusalem was refusing to recognize Kyrillos. That he preferred to discuss in person.

So Tischendorf travelled to Jerusalem, met the grand duke, who was accompanied by his wife and a large retinue, and delightedly escorted the Russian court through the Holy Land. A meeting also took place between the grand duke and the patriarch, but the latter remained wholly unimpressed. He made a few disparaging remarks about Tischendorf's discovery and showed absolutely no inclination to relent where Kyrillos was concerned.

Tischendorf's receipt

Thus the battle over the codex transferred itself from the periphery of the Ottoman Empire to its centre, Constantinople, or, more precisely, to the Bosphorus suburb of Büyükdere, where the Russian ambassador resided. For simplicity's sake, Tischendorf also moved in there for several weeks to assist in obtaining Kyrillos's belated recognition as archbishop, so that he would then be able to convey the Codex Sinaiticus to Russia in triumph. According to Tischendorf, the Russian ambassador of the day, Prince Alexey Lobanov, was highly enthusiastic and promptly set to work on the Ottoman court. The thing was to convince Foreign Minister Fuad Pasha that Archbishop Kyrillos had been legitimately elected, and that he should consequently persuade the patriarch of Jerusalem to recognize his election.

The Sublime Porte, or apex of the Ottoman bureaucracy, was actually persuaded to back Kyrillos, but the Sultan's government hesitated to encroach on the autonomy of the Christian Church and compel the respected Patriarch of Jerusalem to accept him. That left only one means of coercing the patriarch into acceptance: a synod of the Greek Orthodox Churches in Constantinople to which Kyrillos could present his case in person. That would develop into a lengthy affair, however, and Tischendorf was eager to return to Europe with the codex at last. *To wait months on end for the monastery dispute to mature was not to my liking,* he wrote in his late work.[3]

Together with Ambassador Lobanov-Rostovsky, therefore, he came up with a new idea: instead of donating the codex, the monks would first agree to lend it. Lobanov drafted a letter to Archbishop-elect Kyrillos and the rest of the Sinaite fraternity in which he thanked them for the proposed gift and suggested that, until it was actually made, they relinquish the codex to Tischendorf on loan, so that he could work on the manuscript in St Petersburg and publish a printed copy of it. Lobanov's letter further stated: 'In endorsing Herr Tischendorf's request, the Imperial Ambassador expressly states that the said manuscript, if it be lent to the same in St Petersburg, will nonetheless remain the property of the Sinaites until the Superior, in the name of his fraternity, in writing or through the medium of a deputation, shall have formally implemented its donation to the Emperor.'[4]

With Lobanov's letter in his luggage, Tischendorf travelled to Cairo once more. The occupants of the Sinaite monastery there had been following his efforts in Constantinople with keen interest and knew of his endeavours on Kyrillos's behalf, so he received a very cordial welcome. Having suggested to the archbishop-elect and his monks that the codex be lent to St Petersburg for printing purposes, he received the green light after only a short pause for reflection. According to Tischendorf, all the monks present acceded to his request. A document was drafted in which he undertook to return the codex to the monastery as soon as printing was complete.

I, the undersigned, Constantin Tischendorf, currently on a mission to the Near East by order of Alexander II, Tsar of All the Russias, hereby confirm that the Holy Fraternity of Mount Sinai, in accordance with the letter from His Excellency Ambassador Lobanov, has handed me on loan an ancient manuscript of the Old and New Testaments, which is the property of the aforesaid monastery and comprises 346 folia and a small fragment. I shall take this with me to St Petersburg in order to compare the copy previously made by me with the original while the manuscript is being prepared for publication.

The manuscript has been entrusted to me subject to the proviso laid down in the aforesaid letter from Herr Lobanov dated 10. 9. 1859 (No. 510). I undertake to return this manuscript to the Holy Fraternity of Sinai, undamaged and in a good state of preservation, at their earliest request.

Constantin Tischendorf [5]

This document was to play a central role in the subsequent controversy. For now, however, Tischendorf was overjoyed to be able to set off for home with his find. He left Egypt in September 1859 and arrived in St Petersburg in November. His Imperial Majesty received him at the palace of Tsarskoye Selo on 19 November. *The palimpsests, twelve very varied examples of which I was happy to bring with me, aroused the emperor's keenest interest; he took each of them in his hand and ran his searching gaze over the old, faded writing of centuries ago. Later I had the honour of presenting the Codex Sinaiticus to a gathering of the most senior dignitaries of the Russian Church, the holy synod. On 30 November, however, at His Majesty's request, an exhibition of all the manuscripts and antiquities was inaugurated in the magnificent premises of the Imperial Library under the special patronage of its director, Baron Modest von Korff. It was attended with the liveliest interest not only by representatives of the highest social circles but also by simple men of the people. The ancient Sinai Bible outshone all else that was on display.*[6] Tischendorf had attained the zenith of his fame.

Diplomatic arm-twisting

For Tischendorf, the following two-and-a-half years went by in a sort of daze. He wanted – indeed, he *had* – to get the codex printed by autumn 1862 so that he could then present it to the Tsar a second time, as a gift to mark the 1,000th anniversary of the Russian monarchy's foundation. He now invested all his energy in this aim.

First he had to settle how the work would be carried out and make the necessary arrangements. The Russians, who regarded it as a matter of national prestige that the Codex Sinaiticus be published in St Petersburg, offered Tischendorf a well-paid post at St Petersburg University to enable him to devote himself to the great project in peace – from the financial aspect, an extremely tempting proposition. Technologically speaking, they proposed to reproduce the codex by means of a brand-new photographic process. Neither suggestion appealed to Tischendorf. He had no wish to spend the next few years in St Petersburg, far from Saxony, his family, and his familiar surroundings. What mattered to him more, however, was to be able to control the reproduction of the codex himself, and not to have it taken out of his hands by a multitude of ostensible experts in St Petersburg. He had been well served by the Leipzig printing firm of Giesecke & Devrient when publishing his first 43 sheets, and he preferred to stay with them. Instead of experimenting with immature photography, he wanted to bring out the codex by proven, lithographic means, checking until every letter, those of the notes included, was accurately reproduced in every detail.

What aided his opposition to the idea of photography was its great expense. Producing several hundred copies of the codex in the suggested manner would have cost an immense sum of money, so Tischendorf mooted a compromise: St Petersburg would be the printed copies' official place of manufacture, and he himself would merely take batches of parchment sheets to Leipzig and work on them there. A smallish batch could also be processed photographically for experimental purposes. With a heavy heart, Tischendorf passed up the well-paid post in St Petersburg, though not without complaining that his work at Leipzig University was far less well-rewarded. However, since his proposal substantially reduced the cost of the whole project, he eventually got his way.

For the next two years he commuted between Leipzig and St Petersburg – journeys almost as arduous as his treks across the desert to the Sinai monastery. Travelling by horse and carriage or sleigh, and later, too, by rail, he hurried from Saxony to Russia or vice versa, because although the real work took place in Saxony, he could not afford to take his eyes off the St Petersburg arena. He was permanently threatened by disaster because envious individuals and political opponents were intriguing against him in an attempt to scupper his entire project. For various reasons, influential circles at court and within the Orthodox Church had arrayed themselves against Tischendorf.

Certain ministers were afraid that placing his 1,000th-anniversary prestige project under the Tsar's protection, so as to underline Russia's claim to be worldwide Orthodoxy's protecting power, could result in an embarrassing setback because the ownership of the codex was still open to question. Consequently, they wanted to divorce the millennium celebrations completely from the printing of the codex, and, as Tischendorf saw it, downgrade the project into just another academics' playground. He wanted to prevent that at all costs.

Far more dangerous, however, was the hostility of part of the Russian Church. Archimandrite Porfiry Uspensky, the man who had also been to the Sinai monastery before Tischendorf and had held the codex in his hands, wrote a polemic that floored the conservative Tischendorf with arguments of an even more conservative nature.[7] Being naturally resentful of the fact that Tischendorf was causing a stir with the very same manuscript which he had seen but left unexploited because he had failed to discern its importance, he came up with an accusation that initially left Tischendorf speechless: he claimed that the codex was heretical, the work of deviationists who wanted to destroy the Church. Tischendorf could not understand this. He had spent a lifetime toiling through libraries and monasteries in order to prove the literal truth of the Bible and silence impertinent critics of the Holy Scriptures, and now Uspensky was alleging that his work would do precisely what he had always sought to prevent.

The Codex Sinaiticus differed from the Bible in use in Orthodox churches in 1860, not only because its New Testament contained two texts that no longer occurred in the Bible accepted by Uspensky, but also because of sundry deviations in detail. All of Tischendorf's efforts were directed towards eliminating the variations present in different versions of the Bible, whereas Uspensky was doing just the opposite. He described the codex as an attack on his accustomed Bible, which was based on a Byzantine version of the 8th or 9th century. Since his

Bible had to be correct, the authors of the Codex Sinaiticus could only have been dangerous heretics.

In addition to charging that the Codex Sinaiticus omitted to call Jesus the son of God and cast doubt on Mary's immaculate conception, accusations which Tischendorf could easily rebut, Uspensky pointed out that the whole of the end of St Mark's Gospel, which describes the Ascension of Christ, was missing.

Tischendorf naturally deplored this as deeply as Uspensky, but he was not only a theologian who believed in the word of God; above all, he was a palaeographer, a scholar and textual critic. As such, he naturally knew that a 4th-century manuscript carried more weight than a text that had originated several hundred years later. Professional experience had also taught him that, in the course of centuries, *outside hands tend to betray themselves by additions, whereas it is exceptional for something to have been omitted deliberately, that is to say, not because of a mere oversight on the copyist's part.* Tischendorf consequently considered it plain 'nonsense' to charge the Codex Sinaiticus with 'heresy' because of the verses missing from St Mark's Gospel. He put it down to a superstition which cannot admit that reality may sometimes *run counter to our own pious wishes.*[8]

Fortunately for Tischendorf, there were enough experts even in Russia's Orthodox community who endorsed his attitude and thus preserved the Codex Sinaiticus from a heretic's death at the stake.

Uspensky's attack missed its mark, therefore, but his other charge – that the historic manuscript's ownership had not been resolved – remained in the air. Although Tischendorf had been able to ensure that his printed version of the codex be presented to the Tsar on the occasion of the monarchy's 1,000th anniversary, he had been compelled, on the instructions of Golovnin, the Russian minister of education, to delete a reference to this from the title page of the deluxe edition.

When Tischendorf ceremoniously presented it to the Tsar of all the Russias in his palace on 10 November 1862, this read: *Codex Bibliorum Sinaiticus Petropolitanus, removed from the darkness and brought to Europe under the auspices of His Imperial Majesty Alexander II, published by C.T. for the enhancement and glorification of Christian scholarship.*[9]

The fact that Tischendorf called his work the Codex Sinaiticus *Petropolitanus* naturally suggested that the codex had already passed into the Tsar's possession, which was certainly not the case. He justified the designation by pointing out that he had written to Archbishop Kyrillos to ask if he had any objection to it. Having received no reply, he had taken this as his tacit consent.

This was absolutely incorrect, however. Of the several hundred deluxe editions Tischendorf had had printed and the Tsarist court had then distributed to friendly dynasties and major scientific institutions throughout Europe, two had gone to the monastery in Sinai. But instead of enthusiastic congratulations on his wonderful work, all Tischendorf received from the desert was a question: Why hadn't the two copies sent to the monastery been accompanied by the original? In other words, why were the original leaves of the Codex Sinaiticus still in St Petersburg when the purpose of the agreed loan had long been fulfilled? Indeed, why hadn't Constantin Tischendorf wrapped up the codex in its red cloth and brought it back to Egypt? Wasn't that precisely what he had guaranteed the monks in writing?

'True,' says Professor Böttrich of Greifswald, 'but, at the same time, there was talk from the first of presenting the codex to the Tsar as a gift. The receipt Tischendorf left behind for the monks also makes two allusions to the projected gift.' Was Tischendorf therefore at liberty to assume that it would be only a matter of time before the gift was made, so it was nonsensical to deposit the manuscript at the monastery until then? The world of scholarship is divided on these questions to this day. In the 150-odd years that have elapsed since Tischendorf's find, several publications have appeared that either accuse him of theft or defend his actions.

It all began, only a few years after the printing, with a booklet by the Egyptologist Heinrich Brugsch, who travelled the Sinai Peninsula in the 1860s and, of course, visited the monastery. He then published a memoir entitled *Wanderung nach den Türkis-Minen und der Sinai-Halbinsel* [Journey to the Turquoise Mines and the Sinai Peninsula] in which he reported that the monks at the Sinai monastery accused Tischendorf of having swindled them out of their most valuable manuscript.

These reports persisted to such an extent in the ensuing decades that, at the beginning of the 20th century, the American-born successor to Tischendorf's Leipzig chair, Caspar René Gregory, felt it incumbent on him to essay a written rehabilitation of his admired predecessor's reputation.

Tischendorf himself was extremely alarmed by the appearance of Heinrich Brugsch's booklet. He realized that the matter could not be left in the air any longer, and that he must see to it that the gift was formalized. The way in which Brugsch's book *presented the question of the Codex Sinaiticus and my position relative thereto proved to me how advisable it is – indeed, how much I owe it to myself – to work towards a conclusion,*[10] he wrote later.

Accordingly, in the spring of 1869, Tischendorf set off once more for St Petersburg. In the meantime, however, dramatic changes had taken place in Sinai of which he was clearly ignorant. Although Archbishop-elect Kyrillos had been able to present his request in person to the holy synod of the Orthodox Church in autumn 1859, as suggested by Tischendorf and the then Russian ambassador in Constantinople, and had received the assent of nearly all the princes of the Church, the Patriarch of Jerusalem continued to be obstructive. Not even the combined pressure of the other patriarchs and Russian diplomats had induced Patriarch Kyrill to consecrate Kyrillos of Sinai. So Kyrillos remained an archbishop devoid of final recognition and, thus, of only limited competence. When he saw that even Russian influence was insufficient to secure his office, he gradually withdrew from the donation project. 'Tischendorf,' says Professor Böttrich, 'had obviously backed the wrong horse.'

Added to this came another dramatic development. The newly established state of Romania, which had meantime gained its independence from the Ottoman Empire, nationalized Fistizios, Kyrillos's monastery in Wallachia, together with every other church estate – and that was precisely what Kyrillos had been elected to prevent. Apparently, though the circumstances are not entirely clear, Kyrillos came to an arrangement with the new government and pocketed a substantial indemnity. Suspected thereafter of treachery, profiteering and corruption, he suffered a dramatic loss of support among his fellow monks. This being so, he had no wish to expose himself to a charge of having peddled the famous Codex Sinaiticus to the Russians in exchange for filthy lucre.

When Tischendorf got back to St Petersburg in the spring of 1868, it was borne in on him that enthusiasm for the codex had waned considerably. People had other concerns. The Tsar's reform projects had stalled and money was scarce. The new ambassador to the Sublime Porte was General Nikolay Ignatiev, a diplomat who could not slough off his military background and operated with a crowbar rather than diplomatic finesse. Like Tischendorf, Ignatiev regarded the unconsummated donation as an ugly stain upon the white waistcoat of the Russian Empire. He also wanted to bring the matter to a conclusion – not, as certain ministers in St Petersburg were demanding, by giving the codex back to the Sinaites, but by stepping up the pressure on them to make over the valuable item finally and formally. In St Petersburg, Ignatiev had been forced to acknowledge, long before Tischendorf, that in view of the sums the printing had swallowed and the travelling expenses made available to him, the relevant ministries were unprepared to fork out another largish sum in return for the 'gift'. Ignatiev himself had at first thought 25,000 roubles an appropriate recompense, but the Russian court would not hear of it.

So Ignatiev and the Russian diplomats stationed in Alexandria and Jerusalem proceeded to make it clear to the Sinaites, in drastic terms, that they must either surrender the manuscript in return for a considerably smaller sum or forfeit the Tsar's protection and brave all the consequent disadvantages. The Greek scholar Nicholas Fyssas, who has unearthed some of this correspondence in the monastery's archives, makes it clear that the Russians exerted massive pressure on the Sinaite fraternity.[11]

In 1866, not that Tischendorf heard about it, Russian threats, defeat in Romania and the loss of Fistizios Monastery together with the associated suspicion of corruption, led eventually to Archbishop Kyrillos being deposed by his brothers. After the office had remained vacant for some time, they chose Kallistratos, a monk from within their own ranks, to be his successor. Kallistratos was clearly a better choice than Kyrillos because no one doubted his integrity, so this time recognition by Constantinople and consecration by the Patriarch of Jerusalem were easily obtained within a few months. Tischendorf learnt of this at St Petersburg in 1868. With his blessing, Ignatiev made a final and ultimately successful attempt to persuade the imperial bureaucracy to earmark some money as a thank-you for the donation. As the Sinaites' new archbishop, Kallistratos was clearly keen to reestablish relations with the Tsarist empire on a friendly footing, so he finally approved the 'gift' in return for 9,000 gold roubles. At a conservative estimate, this equates to 300,000 euros in today's money.

Nevertheless, doubts about the legitimacy of this transaction remained and still remain. In an essay written in 1964, the late Professor Ihor Sevcenko of Harvard drew attention to certain inconsistencies that raise questions to this day. The central point is that, in the ten years between the codex's discovery by Tischendorf and its relinquishment to the Tsar, the monks of Sinai never committed themselves in writing to making a gift of it. Even years after the gift eventually took place, the relevant document still lacked the signatures of the St Catherine's authorities, although the archbishop and the Cairo monastery authorities had given their consent. In the meantime, the deed of gift itself completely disappeared. The Sinaites assert to this day that no copy of it exists within the monastery, and the document had also disappeared from the Russian archives. It has since reappeared, however. Three years ago, the Russian scholar Anna W Zaharova published an article in which she describes the rediscovered document. According to this, it is signed by the monks of Sinai.[12]

Who owns ancient works of art?

Questions of detail apart, however, the debate over the Codex Sinaiticus is ultimately the same as that which affects the celebrated head of Queen Nefertiti (now to be seen in Berlin) or the frieze from the Athenian Parthenon (in London) and many, many other works of classical antiquity or earlier, most of them 'discovered' in the 19th century by European researchers and borne off to museums in Western Europe and, later on, the United States. In nearly every case they obtained forms of permission whose validity is often disputed today, but straightforward grave-robbing also took place. For instance, Heinrich Schliemann illegally smuggled Priam's Treasure, now held in Moscow after being looted by the Red Army, out of the Ottoman Empire. But even if the excavators of the time could claim to have official documentation, the way this originated remains debatable. Egyptians, Greeks and Turks now insist that such works of art belong back in their places of origin – that they should not be viewed in isolation in some far-off museum, but embedded in the environment in which they came into being.

There are arguments that run counter to this position. For one thing, it is objected that the artefacts were legally acquired, formally speaking, so no one is entitled to ask for them back. For another, it is argued that their removal to Europe was justified because it was the only way such treasures could be preserved for humanity. Constantin Tischendorf repeatedly pointed out what a wretched condition the precious Codex Sinaiticus was in when he discovered it. Even though his assertion that he saved this incomparable relic of early Christian history from ending up in the fire was a blatant subterfuge, it cannot be denied that at the time when he turned up at St Catherine's Monastery, the codex was already disintegrating, and that parts of it were clearly being used for binding more recent books. We cannot tell how much of it would be left today, therefore, if Tischendorf had not brought the sheets of parchment back to Europe.

'Besides,' says Professor Böttrich, 'in rendering the codex utilizable by scholarly research, Tischendorf achieved an immense amount which the monks of Sinai, who are not a scholarly order, would never have achieved.' Last but not least, the Tsarist court expended substantial sums on making the Codex Sinaiticus accessible to Christians in the West. 'Why should the monks of Sinai, who have paid no regard to the earliest evidences of Christianity over the centuries, possess a greater moral right to the codex than European libraries?'

But there is yet another dimension to the debate over the return of ancient works of art, one that is seldom mentioned in Europe. The great, outstanding museums of today resemble cathedrals of the secularized modern age, temples in which human beings pay homage to their own history. What would these temples be – the Louvre, the British Museum, and Museum Island in Berlin – if their greatest works of art disappeared and found their way back to Egypt, Greece and Turkey? It is more than a matter of prestige, after all. Anyone who has seen the hordes of Japanese tourists in the Louvre knows that the most important museums are beacons of modern culture – and, at the same time, sources of foreign exchange.

The countries of origin of Nefertiti & Co would naturally like to tap into this. Athens has recently opened an Acropolis Museum in which space has been left for those portions of the famous Parthenon frieze now in the British Museum, which are only waiting to be replaced *in situ*. The Egyptians aim to build a new museum and future home for Nefertiti in the Valley of the Kings, and the Turkish government is planning a big museum beside the Dardanelles for the Troy treasures. The longtime director of the Troy excavations, the late Professor Manfred Korfmann, developed a scheme for this that may help to neutralize questions of ownership. He based it on rotating exhibitions, replicas and reciprocal loans.

In recent years, the British Library has shown how a dispute over the physical possession of a historic artefact, in this case the Codex Sinaiticus, can be somewhat defused.

The Book of Books

From parchment to the Internet: www.codexsinaiticus.net

The pages are of translucent delicacy, Constantin Tischendorf rhapsodized over the aesthetic appearance of the Codex Sinaiticus when he held the first of it in his hands in 1844. The parchment leaves of the Sinaiticus do indeed radiate an austere beauty. In 2009, when I was able for the first time to inspect an original page of this ancient manuscript in the desert monastery in Sinai, I was moved by its crisp, clear calligraphy from the past. We have only a very vague conception of the life of the people from the period when this text was written down nearly 1,700 years ago. What sort of man – we can fairly safely assume it was not a woman – was the scribe? Was he a person inspired by personal faith or a professional who was paid for his work? Was this copy really produced at the behest of the Roman Emperor Constantine, and did the scribe really sit with several colleagues in Bishop Eusebius's scriptorium in Caesarea, in Alexandria or even Rome?

Many scholars consider the port of Caesarea in Palestine to be the codex's most likely place of origin. The bishop of Caesarea was Eusebius, then the priest on closest terms with Emperor Constantine, who, as head of the Roman Empire, was setting out to adorn his new capital, Constantinople, with prestigious buildings and churches. For these churches Constantine wanted uniform Bibles, and Bishop Eusebius was to have them made. Tischendorf was the first to speculate that the Codex Sinaiticus might be the last surviving example of these imperial Bibles. Someone who has spent years studying the origins of the codex is Professor Harry Y Gamble of Virginia University in the United States. He does not believe that the Codex Sinaiticus is one of the Bibles commissioned by Constantine. Speaking at a British Library conference on the Codex Sinaiticus held in London in the

In order to make parchment out of animal skin, the hide was
stretched on a frame and shaved to render it as thin as possible.

summer of 2009, he posited another theory.[1] According to him, the codex was commissioned by a kind of 4th-century Bill Gates, in other words, a very wealthy man. The reasons for this were primarily practical. The Codex Sinaiticus originated at exactly the same period as the church Bibles for Constantinople, but its size and bulk would have made it too unwieldy and impractical for use in a church.

The church Bibles, Gamble believes, must have been smaller and probably less expensive to produce. The leaves of the Codex Sinaiticus are 38 centimetres high and 34.5 centimetres wide. If one puts the missing text of the Old Testament at around 400 pages, the whole work must once have comprised nearly 800. The bound volume would then have been some 40 centimetres thick – too bulky, Professor Gamble believes, to be used as a church Bible. Besides, the cost of manufacture must have been immense. A whole flock of sheep or herd of cattle had to be slaughtered for their hides, whose processing was laborious and thus costly, so the whole volume would have cost as much as a country house.

For all that, Gamble assumes that a work of this magnitude could only have been produced with the approval and support of the Church. Even if a private individual financed and commissioned the work, 'it was backed by the authority of the Church'. Compared to other manuscripts dating from the early centuries AD, which took the form of scrolls (of papyrus or parchment) and have largely survived only as fragments, the Codex Sinaiticus is probably one of the first books ever to have been manufactured in such a large format.

All that existed previously, with the exception of the Codex Vaticanus, which originated at about the same time as the Sinaiticus (and may even have come from the same scriptorium), were codices containing parts of the Bible, for instance Paul's epistles or individual gospels. At the time, therefore, the manufacture of the Codex Sinaiticus was a technological masterpiece. It used up to 300 animal skins, which came from calves as well as sheep. Experts at the British Library and Leipzig University Library are not entirely in agreement as to how the skins were processed in order to obtain the 'translucent delicacy' extolled by Tischendorf. At Leipzig it is assumed that the skin was split, though this is possible only in the case of sheepskin.

Quite regardless of the animal from which the material was taken, every skin had to be carefully checked for quality and pricked so that scribes could maintain a straight line. Above all, they had to plan how to distribute the text over the numerous pages.

Then several scribes settled down with the portion assigned them and began their laborious work. The ink they employed, which had already been in use for hundreds of years, was iron gall, an extract of crushed gallnuts enriched with iron sulphate and water. Although they all strove to produce a uniform appearance, three scribes can now be distinguished, all of whom were evidently instructed to check and if necessary correct each other's work. Thus, almost every page of the codex displays corrections. These relate to errors or inadvertent omissions when copying existing material, but also subsequent emendations, as changes to the text were often made between the 5th and 7th centuries. Textual analysts infer from these corrections that the contents of the codex were worked on until the 12th century. The changes made reflect the theological debates of their time. It also emerges from this that, even if Professor Gamble's theory is correct and the codex was originally produced for a private individual, it must not long afterwards have come into the possession of some community – or monastic fraternity – which put it to theological use.

Biblical scholars now conclude that the codex remained in Caesarea until the 7th century. In 642 the city was captured by Islamic Arabs and ceased to be a Christian centre. It is clear, however, that the fall of Caesarea also betokened the disappearance of the codex. Subsequent corrections adorned with entries made by Greek monks suggest that it was salvaged by a Greek monastery. It is therefore possible that the Codex Sinaiticus was taken to St Catherine's in Sinai after the fall of Caesarea. On the other hand, the codex may already have been in Sinai at that time, because it is conceivable that Emperor Justinian, when fortifying the monastery in the 6th century, presented the monks with the precious manuscript as an inaugural gift.

The first news of the codex in modern times comes from Vitaliano Donati, an Italian scientist who reported in 1761 that he had seen, in St Catherine's Monastery, 'a Bible comprising sheets of handsome, large, thin, square-shaped parchment, written in a fine, flowing hand'. It was evidently still an intact book at that stage, and it was Tischendorf who discovered the first 126 pages of the Old Testament a good 80 years later. Tischendorf's discovery and removal of the Codex Sinaiticus to Leipzig (43 sheets) and St Petersburg (the whole of the 347 sheets still extant in the monastery) did not, however, constitute the end of the ancient manuscript's odyssey.

Stalin's art auction

Once the codex's donation to the Tsar had been authenticated, the manuscript was ceremoniously transferred from the foreign ministry, where it had been temporarily housed, to the Imperial Library. There it was made available not only to visitors but also to textual analysts, who were able to use it in their research. At the beginning of the 20th century it was also photographed, using the process the Russians had already suggested employing for the production of copies in the 1860s. As an additional legitimation of the Tsar's status as the God-given emperor of the Orthodox Church, however, the codex ultimately proved useless. In 1881, Tsar Alexander II was assassinated by a group of student anarchists who supported the liberation of the peasants. The result of his death was that his two successors totally discarded his cautiously reformist line and devoted themselves to the ideology of imperial absolutism. The retrogressive policy of the last two Tsars only accelerated the revolutionary process in poverty-stricken Russia. In 1905, after violent clashes, Tsar Nicholas II was compelled to share power with a parliament. In February 1917 he was forced to abdicate, and the Bolshevik October Revolution, sparked off by the massacre of demonstrators, finally sealed the fate of the thousand-year Tsarist regime. Nicholas and his family were executed in July 1918. Meanwhile, the Codex Sinaiticus survived the tempestuous changes that were taking place in Russia, unscathed but also unnoticed. This state of affairs persisted until the 1930s.

The beginning of Stalin's dictatorship at the end of the 1920s heralded what was probably the most ambitious attempt in human history to transform a backward agrarian society into an industrialized nation.[2] Stalin stopped at nothing to attain this, but neither the terrorizing of the peasants, who opposed collectivization, nor the immense exertions of millions of enthusiastic communists were sufficient to achieve this: the Soviet Union needed foreign exchange in order to buy know-how and machinery from abroad. The international capital market had been closed to Russia ever since the October Revolution. No bank anywhere in the world would lend the revolutionaries around Lenin, Trotsky and Stalin the money to pay for these urgently needed imports, so the Bolsheviks' Politburo soon hit on the idea of selling off the country's 'family silver' – at first, quite literally.

The Romanovs' silver plate and the luxury items from the Tsar's palaces, up to and including the crown jewels, were soon offered for sale at European art auctions. A so-called 'Objects of Value for Foreign Trade Fund' was set up as early as 1920, and in February 1922, on Leon Trotsky's orders, the contents of the Hermitage were put up for sale. The Hermitage in St Petersburg was probably the biggest museum in the world at that time. All the Tsars since Catherine II had busily collected and assembled *objets d'art* that could more than hold their own with other great European art collections. After the Revolution the Hermitage was at first greatly expanded because several private art collections that had previously belonged to the nobility were incorporated in it. But, when the Revolution urgently needed capital, the great sell-off began. The commission appointed by Trotsky confined itself at first to the jewellery section and the most valuable of the Tsars' household effects. In her book *Verkaufte Kultur* [Sold Culture], Elena Solomacha describes how these initial forced sales developed eventually into a systematic selling-off of European high culture.[3] Called in from 1926 onwards, international art dealers from England and Germany arranged large-scale auctions. At the first big sale, which took place in Berlin in 1928, a total of 447 *objets* from the Hermitage came under the hammer.

This caused a sensation, which to some extent anticipates the fate of the Codex Sinaiticus. During the sale, Russian émigrés spotted pictures that were family possessions of theirs and protested fiercely. The paintings were confiscated and a major lawsuit ensued, but the émigrés failed to win their case and their pleas were dismissed on the grounds that it was 'inadmissible to encroach on the sovereignty of a government recognized by Germany'. In other words, the sovereign Soviet government was at liberty to sell whatever it had in its possession or considered to be its property.

This opened the door to further sales. Before long, masterpieces by Raphael, Botticelli, Rembrandt, Rubens, van Eyck and other artists were put up for sale. The Russians swamped the international art market, which had already been weakened by the economic crisis, and prices slumped badly.

Because of the enforced industrialization undertaken by Stalin at the beginning of the 1930s, however, imports essential to increasing production became even more urgently needed. Instead of limiting themselves to classics from the Hermitage, the Russians tried to turn everything into money. It was at this stage that a British antiquarian bookseller appeared on the scene. A man who at first sight, with his steel-rimmed glasses and white goatee beard, bore a startling resemblance to Leon Trotsky, Ernest Maggs had good contacts in Moscow and knew all about the Codex Sinaiticus. He made the Russians an offer, but they were shrewder than they had been at the beginning of their art sales and offered the codex to some prospective American buyers, with the result that Stalin eventually demanded the exorbitant sum of £100,000 from the British.

Since the British government was not exactly rolling in money either, a campaign was launched that turned the Codex Sinaiticus into a national issue. Arguing that the oldest Bible in the world must be rescued from atheistic communists, Prime Minister Ramsay MacDonald, Archbishop Cosmo Lang of Canterbury, and the biblical scholar and former director of the British Museum, Sir Frederic Kenyon, successfully mounted a fundraising campaign. Depression and economic crisis notwithstanding, the British public contributed so generously to 'save the Bible' that far more was collected than expected and the government had to chip in with less than the £50,000 it had planned to pay for the purchase.

On 27 December 1933 all was in readiness. While the Nazis were consolidating their power in Berlin and Stalin was spurring on the peoples of the Soviet Union to set ever higher production records, the Codex Sinaiticus was ceremoniously handed over in London. A British newsreel shows the bundle of parchment from Leningrad, as St Petersburg then was, being handed by Ernest Maggs to Sir George Hill, director of the British Museum, with Sir Frederic Kenyon looking on. The gentlemen can be seen leafing through the stack of parchment sheets in a rather slapdash way that causes modern restorers to shake their heads in horror. In those days, however, people were more trusting: the Codex Sinaiticus was displayed in the British Museum's entrance hall, where members of the public, who had been so committed to the purchase, could view the precious manuscript for themselves. British newspapers reported that a long queue of visitors formed outside the museum every day for weeks.

Word of this even reached far-off Sinai. The monks there, now subjects of an Egyptian king who was just as dependent on Great Britain as on the former colonial power, saw a chance of recovering 'their' manuscript after all. Only one day after the codex had been solemnly handed to the British Museum, a telegram reached London from Archbishop Porphyrios of Sinai in which he pointed out that the true owner of the codex was his monastic community. The British Museum responded by return with a telegram referring the archbishop to the vendor of the codex, the Soviet government. Sir George Hill evidently felt a trifle uneasy, for all that, because he instituted an enquiry of his own into the circumstances surrounding the gift and commissioned a legal opinion from Lord Hanworth, the second most senior judge in England and Wales. As Hill saw it, however, neither the legal opinion nor the enquiry presented any reason for doubting his spectacular acquisition from Russia. All was well, his experts signalled.

Instead of being returned to Sinai, the Codex Sinaiticus was later transferred to the new British Library, founded in 1973 as an institution in its own right, where it is now displayed in the John Ritblat Gallery. The display case is opened once a week and the pages are turned to prevent the writing from being exposed to light for too long.

The forgotten treasure chamber

Those approaching St Catherine's Monastery today will first pass through the garden of which all earlier visitors spoke so highly. Beyond the garden, the route then taken by monks and pilgrims leads first to a guesthouse and then to a forecourt, fringed with tall trees, in which cars belonging to the monastery are parked. A narrow doorway opens into a passage that leads through the massive wall and another doorway, and comes out in a small internal square. It is by way of this passage that the monks enter and leave the monastery.

For tourists who visit the monastery on the days when it is open in the morning, there is another form of access. From the car park, in which buses are parked a good kilometre from the monastery, a dusty road leads below the garden to the north face of the monastery's perimeter wall. This is where visitors like Constantin Tischendorf used to be winched up by rope to the entrance into the monastery's battlements. This entrance is still clearly visible high up in the massive wall, but modern tourists follow a more convenient route. Beneath the overhead entrance, a big breach has been made in the perimeter wall and secured with an imposing gate. The passageway beneath the tower and defensive wall is some ten metres long. Devotional articles from the monastery and tickets of admission can be purchased in a small shop inside the massive wall. Visitors then enter a passageway that leads past the monastery museum to the entrance to the church. They are conducted into the church and also shown the chapel, which was erected, according to legend, over the site of the burning bush in which God first manifested himself to Moses. After that, they visit the museum and leave the monastery by the gate through which they entered the complex. This little tour is strictly separated from the rest of the monastery to avoid disturbing the monks at their work.

Beside the newly installed passageway designed to promote the monastery's touristic development stands the most massive of the towers that form part of the original monastery wall. When repairs to this tower were being undertaken in the mid 1970s, a startling discovery was made. Some stones suddenly crumbled away, and the astonished labourers found themselves looking into a cavity in a part of the tower that should really have been solid masonry. After a light had been brought, they discovered that above the spot where the museum is now situated at ground level was a chamber of whose existence no one in the monastery had any inkling. But the real surprise came when an opening had been made and the first monk ventured into the mysterious chamber. Stored in that dark cubbyhole and completely cut off from the outside world were thousands of sheets of parchment and paper. Coated with centuries of dust, most of them reposed in baskets like the one in which Tischendorf found his first 126 pages of the codex, or were stored in chests. When the monks brought the first sheets out into daylight, they discovered them to be handwritten texts on parchment that none of them could decipher.[4]

The chamber was discovered in 1975. By degrees, the whole find was transferred to the library, where a start was made on examining and sorting the pages. The monks could not manage this on their own, however, so Professor Panayotis Nikolopoulos took over the task of evaluating the find – a years-long task, given that the material weighed a total of 1.5 tonnes. After carrying out a preliminary systematization of the sheets, Professor Nikolopoulos managed to discover why and when the manuscripts had vanished into the tower. The monastery had refurbished its library in 1745. On that occasion, all loose sheets of manuscript in regular use were sorted out and the unused remainder deposited inside the tower, where they were eventually forgotten. While Professor Nikolopoulos was working his way through mountains of ancient fragments, the news that further parts of the Codex Sinaiticus had turned up began to percolate through the international community of Biblical scholars. It was no more than a rumour at first, but then, at a meeting in Vienna in 1981, Archbishop Damianos confirmed the sensational news that another 11 sheets of the famous Codex Sinaiticus had been found in a walled-up chamber together with some smaller textual fragments. Several more years went by before scholars from outside the monastery set eyes on the sheets. This time the monks guarded their treasure jealously, its immense value being common knowledge.

In the 1990s, therefore, the community of biblical scholars was confronted by the following situation: the bulk of the extant 4th-century manuscript, 347 sheets, was in the possession of the British Library; 43 sheets were in the strongroom of Leipzig's University Library; and the 11 sheets most recently discovered were in Sinai. There also existed in the Russian National Library in St Petersburg some very small fragments that had not accompanied the rest to London in 1933, and further fragments were turning up in the Sinai monastery bit by bit, parts of the codex having been used in the 18th century as binding material for newly-bound volumes (usually for reinforcing the covers). It could therefore be assumed that a systematic search of the entire monastery library would bring further fragments to light. Thus, any scholars who wanted to examine the whole of the Codex Sinaiticus faced a difficult task: they had to travel halfway round the world and obtain permission to work with material from four different institutions – a downright impossible undertaking.

Nor, in the mid-1990s, could this state of affairs be expected to change in the foreseeable future. Although the monks still insisted that the manuscript should be reunited in its entirety at their monastery, they had no realistic chance of achieving this. The donation may be valid in purely legal terms; at any rate, it is unlikely that any court in London or Leipzig will order the British Library or Leipzig University Library to surrender the manuscript. Government pressure is equally improbable, because Egypt has been campaigning, if at all, for the relinquishment of important exhibits from the pharaonic tombs. Islamic Cairo regards a Christian manuscript as something of lesser importance. As for the Orthodox Church, it will be unable to generate a public mood, in either Britain or Germany, that could compel the relevant institutions to relinquish it 'voluntarily'.

It was in the year 2000, against this background, that the British Library made an innovative suggestion: instead of continuing to dispute the physical possession of the Codex Sinaiticus, why not create a virtual edition of it, accessible to all and incorporating every last snippet of the manuscript, no matter how small?

The project

The British Library in Central London looks rather unspectacular from the outside. Ochre-brown in colour, the building is such a rabbit warren that its true dimensions cannot be grasped at first sight. Once through the glass doors, however, visitors find themselves in an entrance hall that already conveys the feeling that they are in one of the biggest treasure houses of knowledge in the world. The galleries and walkways, which give access to one room after another, attain a giddy height. Founded by an Act of Parliament in 1973, the British National Library moved into its brand-new premises in 1998. It houses 150 million books, periodicals, maps, and other forms of stored information, and boasts of possessing more first editions and other valuable items than any other library in the world.[5]

One of these special items is the Codex Sinaiticus. The original of the precious manuscript is kept in the Ritblat Gallery, a room accessible from the entrance hall, where it reposes in a display cabinet. Otherwise than in 1933, when the codex came to London from Leningrad, it no longer consists of a collection of loose sheets – the curators of the British Museum rebound it into book form; more precisely, into two volumes, one containing as much of the Old Testament as still exists, and the other the complete New Testament.

Around the turn of the millennium, associates of the library evolved the idea of rendering the codex universally accessible with the aid of modern technology. As a result, one of the oldest manuscripts in the world became the subject of a large-scale editorial and research project designed to liberate the text from the constraints of its scattered parchment leaves and present it on the Internet in such a way that a transcription of the codex and English, German, modern Greek and Russian translations would be available for downloading.[6] This entailed photographing and digitizing all the extant pages and fragments. In addition, the project envisaged curatorially processing each sheet, that is to say, closely examining and describing it. For this purpose the British team compiled an extensive list of questions which they went through, page by page, in the years that followed.

'It was rather difficult to begin with,' says Juan Garcés, a Spaniard who studied theology in Germany, made his career in South Africa, and joined the Codex Sinaiticus project in 2005. The British adopted a rather casual approach at first, and that did not go down well with St Catherine's Monastery in particular. 'We needed more diplomatic finesse than we initially realized,' Garcés concedes. Although it was easy to agree on an international research project with Leipzig University, and the National Library in St Petersburg could soon be brought aboard, the monks from the Sinai Desert proved somewhat more difficult. The British wanted to send someone to photograph the additional pages of the Codex Sinaiticus found in St Catherine's Monastery, just like that, as if it had never been a bone of contention at all. A lot of proverbial china was smashed and relations with Sinai had to be repaired before the London authorities realized that they could not implement the project like any other research project – not with the monks of St Catherine's. The director travelled to Egypt and paid his respects to Archbishop Damianos in person. The latter stipulated that, in addition to digitization, the history of the Codex Sinaiticus must be investigated thoroughly enough for all the institutions involved to be able to agree on a common form of words.

In March 2005 an agreement to cooperate was formally signed. As well as the then director of Leipzig University Library, Dr Ekkehard Henschke, and the deputy director of the Russian National Library, Dr Alexander Bukreyev, His Holiness Archbishop Damianos travelled to London in person. Progress thereafter in London and Leipzig was rapid, but cooperation with the monastery continued to be poor. This was due less to the monks' scepticism, however, than to a lack of equipment and the monastery's isolated location, which remains relatively inaccessible.

One case in point was that a photographer who had come specially from the United States, complete with all the equipment he needed in order to digitize 11 pages, had to leave without accomplishing anything because the pages were not made available to him. To the monks, the manuscript's digitization and curatorial evaluation are significantly less important than clarifying the historical events surrounding its removal to Europe. There has also been a certain amount of haggling about financial payments, just as there was, albeit on a larger scale, when the donation was in progress. As compensation for cooperating in the joint digitization process, the monastery had been promised funds within the context of the research project to enable its library to be expanded and modernized in keeping with the latest technological developments. When I visited the monastery in January 2009, modern photographic and digitization equipment had been installed, but the promised renovation of the library was still hanging fire. Whereas Russian and German experts set to work to compile as detailed a history of the codex as possible, especially for the period 1859–69, the phase in which Tischendorf took the sheets with him to St Petersburg and negotiations over the gift were in progress, Greek experts at the monastery, but also in the relevant archives in Cairo, were searching for documents that could support the monks' version and bring about the return of the codex to Sinai after all. The contract for formulating a valid version of the history of the Codex Sinaiticus was then awarded, at Leipzig's suggestion, to Professor Christfried Böttrich of Greifswald.

The Book of Books on the Internet

'The significance of the digitization of the Codex Sinaiticus consists not only in its defusing of the dispute over ownership; it is also an important pilot project for libraries of the future in general,' says Professor Ulrich Johannes Schneider. Professor Schneider is the present director of Leipzig University Library and, as Dr Henschke's successor, the inheritor, so to speak, of the Codex Sinaiticus project. His institution has not only curatorially examined, then scanned and digitized its own 43 sheets, but also taken over the technical side of the project. It was Leipzig that developed the website on which the codex can now be retrieved, and Leipzig is the site of the servers through which the famous manuscript is available worldwide.

Years of laborious work preceded this. Leipzig University Library's senior curator, Ute Feller, gives a vivid description of how each of the 43 sheets was removed from the strongroom and examined. They were then photographed by means of a special process. For the description of the sheets the London curators had prepared a list of questions in over 150 categories, each of which had to be carefully answered for every sheet. Contrary to the British, Ute Feller believes that most of the sheets consist of sheepskin that was split to produce especially fine, thin parchment. Absolute certainty is impossible, however, 'because nobody wants to sacrifice a piece of parchment to carry out a DNA test,' she says. With work on the codex already in progress, Professor Schneider regularly visited London to participate in discussions concerning the project. In addition to technical questions, these concerned the presentation of the work.

Leipzig's first great day dawned in July 2008. London had agreed that the website, insofar as it was finished, should be given an airing on the Internet so that errors could be eliminated and improvements made before the whole project was officially completed a year later. Addressing the assembled dignitaries of Leipzig University and the

Professor Dr Ulrich Johannes Schneider, director of Leipzig
University Library, and Father Justin, librarian of St Catherine's
Monastery, compare an original page of the Codex Sinaiticus with
Tischendorf's 19th-century lithographic facsimile edition.

scholarly community of Saxony, the technical coordinator, Zeki
Mustafa Dogan, explained how it was supposed to work.

Ulrich Johannes Schneider later described the scene as follows:
'When Mustafa Dogan had finished, John Tuck, the project leader
from London, thanked everyone concerned, and especially St Catherine's Monastery, for their cooperation. Colleagues from London and
Birmingham, hooked up by video conference, also delivered brief
speeches, and everything conveyed an impression of great modernity
and technological progress – until the website crashed. The server
went down an hour after switch-on. Having been designed to cope
with 100,000 simultaneous hits, it was quickly upgraded to four times
that capacity, but that was no good either. Nearly 3 million people,
several hundred thousand of them at the same time, had clicked on
the page.'[7]

No one in Leipzig had reckoned with such a mass onslaught. On the second day, therefore, the university's computer centre made its most powerful machine available. That proved sufficient for the time being – until another crash occurred a year later. On 6 July 2009, when it was finally announced, this time on the occasion of the aforesaid conference at the British Library in London, that the world's oldest Bible would be accessible to everyone on the Internet, the servers went down again. Approximately 20 million people worldwide wanted to take a look at the mysterious old manuscript, and not even Leipzig's most powerful computer could cope with that. The page was repeatedly unavailable for the first few days, but this situation has since been rectified. The website functions without interruption and is freely available to the world of scholarship.

What can one actually do with the webpage? Here is Professor Schneider again: 'The website displays the manuscript itself in high-resolution and with almost infinitely enlargeable images. It also gives a scientifically produced transcription that not only faithfully reproduces every line but also picks out the corrections and marks them in blue. The images of the manuscript and the transcriptions are closely connected, every word in the transcription being linked with the corresponding group of characters in the continuously written original text. Clicking on the transcription produces a red frame in the original text, so one can always tell exactly where one is.'

Work on the translations is still in progress. The page is available in all four project languages, but of the Biblical texts themselves only parts can currently be seen on the page in English and German, with Russian and modern Greek to follow later. Information about the project is also available. Since the beginning of 2010, the webpage has included a text on the history of the Codex Sinaiticus.

The diplomatic solution

During the conference in London, Professor Böttrich presented a summary of the results of his research into the history of the Codex Sinaiticus. His audience included Archbishop Damianos and the monastery's chief librarian, Father Justin. The monastery had also sent the archaeologist Nicholas Fyssas into the fray. When both men were finished, it was clear that their interpretations of the past were incompatible. Although Böttrich expressed great sympathy for the monastery's position and the monks' role as guardians of the treasure for centuries, he was ultimately in no doubt that the donation to the Tsar in 1869 had been legally valid, and that to return the manuscript would not be justified. Not so Nicholas Fyssas, who assessed the donation in accordance with how it had, in his opinion, been brought about: by means of massive Russian diplomatic pressure on the monastery. Fyssas had gone through quotations from contemporary correspondence, and in his view they enabled one to conclude that the monks had effectively been coerced into relinquishing the manuscript to the Tsar because they would otherwise have been deprived of the political protection and the not inconsiderable financial assistance accruing to the monastery from Russia. What Fyssas did not say, but doubtless meant, was that the deed of gift had come into being more or less 'unethically'.

Silence prevailed for a while after the two adversaries had said their pieces. In particular, no word of what was to happen reached Professor Böttrich in Greifswald. It was not until late in 2009 that he received from London the news that his text could not go on the website because the monks had withheld their consent. He was not unduly surprised; their dissent had long been in the wind. Improbable though the return of the manuscript to the monastery is, the monks refuse to approve anything in writing that would signify their confirmation of the donation's legality and legitimacy.

Consequently, the project directors were eventually obliged to agree on a version that deliberately left certain questions open: *The text which follows, concerning the history of the Codex Sinaiticus, is the fruit of collaboration by the four Institutions that today retain parts of the said Codex: the British Library, the Library of the University of Leipzig, the National Library of Russia in St Petersburg, and the Holy Monastery of the God-Trodden Mount Sinai (Saint Catherine's). These Institutions recognize that events concerning the history of the Codex Sinaiticus, from 1844 to this very day, are not fully known; hence, they are susceptible to widely divergent interpretations and recountings that are evaluated differently as to their form and essence. Although they have not come into full accord over the recent history of the Codex, the four collaborating Institutions offer the present, common, agreed text as the basis of a common formulation, as a framework of historical reference that may be completed by yet further documents, and as a basis for dialogue and the interpretation of events.*[8]

The ensuing text then makes it clear that events between 1859, when Tischendorf was shown the manuscript in the monastery, and November 1869, when the donation to the Tsar took place, are in need of further clarification. It is also pointed out that in 1933 the monastery had asserted its claim to ownership *vis-à-vis* the British Museum, but that this claim had been rejected on the basis of documents then available in London relating to that very same period of 1859–69.

So the text on the website does not completely exclude the possibility that documents may turn up in the future which would shake the legality of the donation to the Tsar and, thus, render the sale to London equally suspect. In theory, everything is still up in the air; in practice, though, little will change. For the time being, the leaves of the Codex Sinaiticus will remain where they are. The monastery's holding may expand if further fragments are discovered there, but that is all. Besides, digitization and the ability to call it up on the Internet has rendered the Codex Sinaiticus immensely popular, which naturally benefits St Catherine's. Every click enhances the monastery's fame and facilitates fundraising, so a new library will not be the last of the Sinaite monks' benefits. Even today, thanks to the manifold support of its admirers from all over the world, the monastery in the desert has become one of the wealthiest Orthodox retreats on earth. Where their financial future is concerned, at least, the last Byzantines have no cause for concern.

In the Beginning Was the Word
The Codex Sinaiticus and the origins of the Bible

In my own audacious attempts to effect a new treatment of the New Testament, I became convinced that, in order to reproduce the text as it had once left the hand of the writer, the few very ancient documents from the 4th, 5th and 6th centuries are far more important than the many hundreds of documents from later centuries. At the same time, however, I realized that, discounting a few exceptions, very inadequate research had been devoted to the earliest documents in particular. The task of reproducing the original sacred text on which Christianity itself is very largely dependent seemed to me to be one of Christian scholarship's most exalted tasks. I was determined to devote my own energies thereto.[1]

In the last book he wrote before his death, *Die Sinaibibel,* published in 1871, Constantin Tischendorf employs those words to describe the motive underlying his life's work. He had set out to reconstruct Christianity's 'original sacred text', and now, at the end of his life, he was taking stock.

His aim, he wrote, had been *to combat habit.* This habit had *since Erasmus* been *the wonted Greek text of the New Testament, which has also become the basis of the most widespread translations, such as the German, the English, the Russian.* Tischendorf was here referring to Erasmus of Rotterdam, who published his critical edition of the Greek New Testament in Rotterdam in 1516. That text, wrote Tischendorf, *was taken in the 16th century from some newish Greek manuscripts that happened to be available. It turned out to be the one of which thousands of copies had been almost exclusively disseminated in the Byzantine national church for over a thousand years. However, increasingly productive source studies undertaken in the past two centuries have proved that the earliest Greek documents, as well as the Latin, the Syrian, the Egyptian, and others, together with the very numerous citations from the Fathers of the Church, display divergences from the usual printed text that extend to nearly every verse of the New Testament, although most of them are of a purely linguistic nature and carry dogmatic weight only in fairly rare instances.*[2]

In Tischendorf's view, however, these source studies suffered from the disadvantage that the older texts from the 5th and 6th centuries were only fragments, and the Codex Vaticanus, the only surviving example of a 4th-century Bible, predominantly contained texts from the Old Testament with only a few from the New. *But what could be more desirable for this important matter [the source studies, J.G.] than the discovery and publication of a complete New Testament comparable in age and text only to the Codex Vaticanus, hitherto regarded, save for five books, as the finest and most complete? Notwithstanding all the deficiencies inherent in this documentary treasure from Sinai and related documents, it is undoubtedly establishing a new era in textual criticism, even though correct use of the same requires complete textual-historical understanding and a sage and cautious approach. The existence of the Sinai Bible crucially enables us to reconstruct at least one apostolic text that was in widespread use during the second century. It is obvious how much closer this text must be to the apostolic original than any one of later date.*[3]

Although Tischendorf's enthusiasm is understandable from his own point of view, those who have not devoted their lives to textual criticism will find it hard to comprehend. The fact is that the divergences the Codex Sinaiticus displays from the usual, Erasmus-based text of the New Testament are indeed, as Tischendorf himself wrote, of a mainly linguistic nature. Experts may find it sensational that a word or a sentence has often been omitted, but this does not turn the known version of the Bible upside down. Few theologians are excited by even the most striking divergence, the complete omission of the last 11 verses of St Mark's Gospel, in which Jesus's Ascension is recounted in the traditional manner. Even though it is clear from the Codex Sinaiticus that those verses were added to St Mark's Gospel subsequently, the Ascension is described elsewhere in the New Testament, so the subsequent addition is regarded as a venial sin. Consequently, the usual version of the Bible has not been corrected to accord with the Codex Sinaiticus; verses 9–20 of Chapter XVI of St Mark's Gospel continue to appear in every New Testament.

However, the Codex Sinaiticus does elsewhere display a divergence from the prevailing norm which is far more important than any detailed textual variations. The Sinai Bible contains two New Testament books that are entirely missing today: the so-called Epistle of Barnabas and the Shepherd of Hermas, two texts that were later rejected as being apocryphal, false and unholy sources. This does, however, raise an extremely interesting point, namely, that different versions of the New Testament existed until well into the 4th century. Being an expert on early Christianity, Tischendorf naturally knew that the development of the New Testament was a longish process. He had also known of the existence of those two old apocryphal texts but was acquainted with only Latin fragments of them. It is surprising, therefore, that he did not attribute any fundamental value to these discoveries, for what their presence in the Codex Sinaiticus cogently demonstrates is that the original New Testament text which Tischendorf was so urgently seeking did not exist at all as a whole. That was why Tischendorf himself remarked that the Codex Sinaiticus might render it possible *to reconstruct at least one apostolic text that was widespread during the second century.*

As we know today, there were very many more so-called apostolic texts than appear in the New Testament, but why and in what way were some texts picked out as being 'sacred sources' while others were rejected? Tischendorf's response to this question is only oblique. He considered the four canonical gospels of the New Testament, the Acts of the Apostles, The Revelation of St John the Divine, and the epistles of Paul and others, which now form the canon of the New Testament, to be authentic apostolic texts. What he was actually seeking was the earliest version of the four gospels. He believed that the selected gospels had actually been written by the apostles, the personal companions and eye-witnesses of Jesus, or at least by associates of theirs who could base their accounts on the testimony of an apostle. This is why he sought to prove that these texts had been written back in the 1st century, and actually by disciples of Jesus. Employing a complicated chain of evidence, he thought he could demonstrate that a phrase in the Epistle of Barnabas, one of the two apocryphal books he discovered in the Codex Sinaiticus, proved that Mark's gospel was written before the turn of the 1st century.[4] And if one of the four gospels could be proved to have originated at that early date, the same – Tischendorf believed – must apply to the other three. He was convinced that the four gospels *must already have been in use at the close of the first century.*

To the modern observer it seems certain that Tischendorf's research into the origin of the gospels far from answered all outstanding questions, and that, in consequence, he could not prevent further critical questions from being raised. After all, even if the texts really did originate at the end of the 1st century, it remains wholly uncertain who actually wrote them. Those who devote themselves to the Bible with scholarly exactitude cannot depend on achieving the result they desire.

Was it really eyewitnesses of a historical Jesus who wrote down the four gospels, and is that why those stories still constitute the core of the New Testament today? Even if that were so, the question remains as to who determined the New Testament's composition and laid it down that the Epistle of Barnabas and the Shepherd of Hermas, for example, were apocryphal texts? The discovery of the Codex Sinaiticus poses more questions than it answers.

Genesis of a book

Although I grew up in a devout Protestant family, such questions played no part in my everyday or community life. As a youngster, I was far more interested in Marxist analyses of capital than in 2,000-year-old Biblical texts, so they didn't feature in my studies either. If any theology interested me, it was the liberation theology of Latin America. When I first applied myself to Tischendorf's Codex Sinaiticus, therefore, I presupposed that the canon of the New Testament must have been laid down by some act of ecclesiastical policy. And since the first ecumenical council of Nicaea, convoked by Emperor Constantine in 325, is generally regarded as the early Church's most important gathering, I assumed that the decision had been taken then.

I was all the more surprised when I came to immerse myself in the records of that historic episcopal conference. It appeared that the Church was then preoccupied exclusively with the question of whether Jesus was God or man; of the same substance as God, or only a man, like his father, Joseph. Arius, a priest from Alexandria, caused a furore with his theory that, being the Son of God, Jesus must be subordinate to Him, so he could not be like Him. This dispute threatened to prevent the unification of the Church to which Constantine aspired for political reasons, so he pressed the bishops for a consensual ruling. The records of the first ecumenical council contain a lot of interesting material, but one looks in vain for any discussion, let alone decisions, as to which New Testament texts were binding upon Christians. Why wasn't this a subject for debate, when differently constituted New Testaments still existed decades later and Christians from different cities and countries invoked altogether different 'original texts'? After intensive study, I have in fact realized that the canonical development of the New Testament is one of the most fascinating and still not fully clarified processes in religious history.

Countless papers on this subject have been published in the century-and-a-half since Tischendorf's day. In essence, I have confined my reading to those that embody the latest state of research. One extremely productive source of information on the canonical development of the New Testament is the books by Professor Gerd Theissen of Heidelberg.[5] The first attested reference to the complete list of the 27 books of the New Testament occurs in the Easter letter of Bishop Athanasius of Alexandria in 367, 42 years after the Council of Nicaea. There is no earlier source that mentions them in their entirety. The Codex Sinaiticus, which was probably already written by that time, included the Shepherd of Hermas and the Epistle of Barnabas, to which Bishop Athanasius's Easter letter makes no reference. This list was binding only on the diocese of Alexandria, however; in other regions other bishops laid down what should and should not be read. 'For all that,' writes Gerd Theissen, 'the extent of the canon was broadly established by the end of the 2nd century, discounting a few texts, although there was no central institution in the 2nd century that could have decided which texts communities should refer to.' Canonical development is thus 'a historical enigma'.

The basis of the canon was the decision in favour of the four gospels according to Matthew, Mark, Luke and John. Originally, it was probably the case that in certain communities one gospel was read and that community traced its origins back to that apostle from whom the gospel stemmed. But that was only the second step. In the beginning was the word, not the text. Christianity was originally a religion passed on by word of mouth. The earliest records were so-called collections of sayings attributed to Jesus. There were also reports of Christ's Passion. People began to write down salvational histories of Jesus to demarcate them from their non-Christian surroundings. Besides, writing was so much the done thing, both by the Jews and by their Greek neighbours, that educated people were unwilling to forgo it, especially when it emerged that the early Christians' expectation that Jesus would return as the Messiah and redeem the world during their lifetime failed to materialize as the years went by, so they had to reckon with a longer sojourn on earth.

One of the reasons why the four above-named gospels ultimately prevailed over various other salvational histories written in the 2nd century was that they were among the earliest written evidence of the activities in Palestine of the itinerant preacher named Jesus. On the basis of extant letters from early bishops, detailed textual analysis and our present knowledge of the political and social situation in Palestine at the beginning of our era, it is now assumed that the earliest of the four gospels is the so-called Gospel according to St Mark, which was probably written in about AD 70. One reason for this assumption is that the Romans' destruction of the Great Temple in Jerusalem is already mentioned in St Mark's Gospel. Jerusalem and the Temple were almost totally razed to the ground in the year 70. Matthew and Luke come next, both probably written between the years 80 and 90, followed by St John's Gospel, written around the turn of the century and the most recent story of Jesus to have made it into the New Testament canon.

The authors of the New Testament

But were the authors of these gospels actually companions of the historical figure named Jesus in the Bible? The Catholic theologians Katharina Cemin and Jürgen Werlitz vividly summarize the latest state of research into this question in their book *Die Verbotenen Evangelien* [The Forbidden Gospels], published in 2007.[6] According to this, although early Christians assumed that Mark had at least an indirect relationship with Jesus, the facts belie it. It emerges from a work by Bishop Papias of Hierapolis (now Pamukkale in Turkey) dating from AD 130 that Mark seemed to be a companion of the apostle Peter. He would thus have acquired his knowledge not from direct personal experience but as the disciple of an apostle.

'However, closer analysis of Mark's gospel compels one to conclude that too much of the evidence militates against this theory,' say Ceming and Werlitz. Mark was unfamiliar with the geography of Palestine, and his theological approach tends to suggest that he was not a Jewish convert to Christianity.

One must also bear in mind that, although it has often been suppressed in the history of the Christian churches, Jesus, if he existed, is known to have been a Jew like the earliest adherents he gathered around him on his wanderings through Samaria and Judaea. Thus the earliest Christian community after his execution consisted of Jews who espoused his teachings. They are known in literature as Jewish Christians – as opposed to heathen Christians, or non-Jews who later found their way to Christianity. At first, however, Jesus's adherents were simply one Jewish sect among others desirous of reforming Judaeism.

Scholars are largely in agreement that the crucial step on the road from a small Jewish sect to a world religion was taken by St Paul, the missionary and preacher. The Jew Saul, a Roman citizen from Tarsus, a town beside the Mediterranean in what is now Turkey, experienced an 'awakening' in which Jesus appeared to him in a vision, transforming him from Saul, a persecutor of Jewish Christians, into Paul, an ardent devotee of Christ's teachings. It was this Jew who ultimately saw to it that Christianity did not lapse into oblivion as one Jewish sect among others. He ensured that adherents of heathen religions, too, could convert to Christianity without undergoing the circumcision prescribed by Judaeism or having to adhere to its strict rituals concerning food, cleanliness and the Sabbath.

Paul achieved this in the face of fierce opposition from the Jewish Christian community in Jerusalem and thereby created the precedent that non-Jews could also become Christians. In so doing, he opened up Christianity to a Mediterranean world that was predominantly Greek. Hellenistic Greek had been the *lingua franca* of the eastern Mediterranean ever since Alexander's campaigns in 300 BC. The Jewish Christians spoke Aramaic, but Mark, like the authors of all four gospels, wrote in Greek. His readers were heathen Christians, so he explained Jewish terms and customs for their benefit. Mark's gospel was probably written in Syria, already far removed in both time and space from the itinerant preacher in Palestine. Thus the author or authors of Mark's gospel are more likely to have been acquainted with Paul than Peter, and we know that Paul, whose epistles are the earliest written testimony to Christianity, experienced Jesus only as a vision.

What applies to Mark applies equally to Matthew and Luke. The authors of those two gospels also wrote in Greek, and both used Mark as one of their sources. But why should eyewitnesses have used a non-eyewitness as a source? Biblical scholars are now unanimous that these two authors used another already existing version of Jesus's sayings in addition to Mark's Gospel, since they both quote similar pronouncements by Jesus of which Mark was evidently ignorant (the so-called 'Q Source').[7]

Ceming and Werlitz consider the likeliest supposition to be that Matthew's gospel was written in a Jewish Christian community in the Diaspora, or somewhere in the region of Syria. The author of Luke's gospel, on the other hand, was a non-Jewish Christian who wrote for non-Jewish Christians and held the Jews responsible for crucifying Jesus. His gospel could already have been written in Rome.

The three so-called synoptic gospels are mutually referential and distinguished by a similar course of events in the story of Jesus, unlike the last of the four canonical gospels. John's gospel is considerably more abstract than the other three. Assigning only a small role to the historical Jesus, he describes the 'post-Easter Son of God'. To quote Ceming and Werlitz: 'Its radical rejection of the Jewish conception of the law and detachment from Jewish customs, but also linguistic clues such as the translation of Aramaic terms, prompt one to conclude that John's gospel was addressed to a community which was no longer rooted in Jewry.'

The last to be written, this gospel was widely disseminated on the west coast of Asia Minor, particularly in Ephesus. Legend has it that Bishop Polycarp of Smyrna, now Izmir, actually knew John, the disciple of Jesus. Be that as it may, Polycarp's enthusiasm for John's gospel is said to have greatly contributed to its inclusion in the New Testament canon along with the synoptic gospels.

The selection process

As Gerd Theissen relates, what clinched the selection of the four gospels as the nucleus of what later became the New Testament was that the community in Rome and the communities in Asia Minor, then the most important centres of early Christianity, agreed on those particular four.

The second reason was a common front against the 'first heretics'. One such was Marcion, who came from Asia Minor to Rome and caused a sensation there in AD 140. Marcion completely rejected the Old Testament because he could see no connection between the God of the Old Testament and the God of love preached by Jesus. Having split the Roman community with his doctrine, he founded a church of his own and accorded sole validity to Luke's gospel.

Consequently, the majority church began to define its identity partly by differentiating itself from Marcionism. In Rome this included referring to at least three gospels in active use there, namely those of Matthew, Mark and Luke. John's gospel was either not known or not popular in the early Roman community. This situation did not change until it endeavoured to join forces with the principal communities of Asia Minor. The question to be settled was when to celebrate Easter. In Rome, Easter was celebrated according to the chronology of the synoptic gospels, in which Jesus's resurrection occurs after the Jewish Passover, whereas Christians in Asia Minor adhered to John's gospel, in which the resurrection takes place before it. In the year 155, therefore, Rome hosted a summit meeting at which the communities of Asia Minor were represented by Bishop Polycarp and that of Rome by Bishop Anicetus.

Although the participants did not agree on a common point in time, they pragmatically decided that both junctures were possible. This indirectly placed John's gospel on a par with the three synoptic gospels in Rome as well, and people grew accustomed to all four becoming basic constituents of the community's scriptures. Furthermore, both community representatives agreed that Marcion should be rejected as a 'heretic'. 'This,' Theissen believes, 'is why one is justified in supposing that the four-gospel canon became a mark of orthodoxy, because Marcion recognized only one gospel. John's gospel, which was only unenthusiastically adopted in Rome, became more acceptable because of the common front against Marcion.' [8]

All the other gospels in the extensive Jesus literature of the 2nd century failed to gain acceptance because they possessed only regional significance, being read primarily on the east Mediterranean seaboard, and did not feature in the compromise between Rome and Asia Minor. However, Theissen is convinced that there were also intrinsic reasons for this. The best-known apocryphal or 'hidden' gospel, the Gospel of Thomas, had only a local focus in eastern Syria. But apart from this local, marginal position, writes Theissen, 'it was a gospel of the solitary, not a basic book for a community. It advocates an individualistic form of mysticism and, in the light of that mysticism, lends the recorded words of Jesus a mysterious aura.' That is why it remained a gospel recognized only by small groups in the East. [9]

When the Church subsequently outlawed these gospels as 'forbidden scriptures', a whole collection of them was buried in the Egyptian desert. In December 1945, in a graveyard near the small town of Nag Hammadi in Lower Egypt, Egyptian peasants discovered a large earthenware jar containing several copies of these forbidden scriptures. They are codices like the Codex Sinaiticus, or leather-bound collections of leaves. To date, 13 collections of manuscripts have been evaluated, these being Coptic translations of Greek writings of the 2nd and 3rd centuries. The Nag Hammadi finds round off our picture of the rejected gospels and illustrate, yet again, what a wealth of materials the Fathers of the Church had to draw on when putting their Bible together.

There can never have been an 'Urtext', therefore, and it is more than doubtful whether the authors of today's canonical gospels ever knew a historical Jesus. Constantin Tischendorf's quest for the apostles' historical text ultimately achieved the opposite of what he was seeking to prove. Instead of reconstituting an original text, historico-critical Biblical scholarship, of which he himself was a part, has more and more clearly shown how diverse Christian currents of thought already were in the 2nd century AD, and how tortuous were the routes to the development of a majority church with a recognized canon of 'Holy Scriptures'.

Success

In 1871, Tischendorf naturally took a different view. As he saw it, he had fulfilled his own mission and could complete the critical edition of the Greek New Testament on which he had been working all his life. In 1859 he had gone to the Sinai monastery with a 7th revised edition; thereafter, with the Codex Sinaiticus in his baggage, he could proceed to complete his task. The last revised edition of his Greek New Testament appeared in two volumes in 1869 and 1872. In notes on almost every page of those two volumes, Tischendorf set out all the variant readings he had researched in 30 years of studying ancient manuscripts. As a rule, he gave preference to the Codex Sinaiticus versions.

Tischendorf was thus a theological pioneer. His edition of the Greek New Testament has now been superseded by versions inclusive of new findings, but 'without Tischendorf,' Christfried Böttrich writes in his capacity as a professor of theology, 'these editions would be quite inconceivable. Tischendorf's research in the 19th century laid the foundations on which our modern editions of the Bible – both the original Greek texts and their translations – are based.'

At the time, many of Tischendorf's colleagues did not take as favourable a view of his work as Böttrich does in retrospect. Although he was Leipzig University's most celebrated figurehead, other members of the faculty thought little of the great itinerant scholar. The whole faculty attempted to block his first appointment to an extraordinary professorship of theology in 1845. They adjudged his first edition of the Greek New Testament 'a total blunder', but his appointment was imposed from above by the minister of education and ultimately by the court of Saxony, to which he felt a close attachment. The post was his reward for the first 43 leaves of the Codex Sinaiticus, which he had brought back with him from Sinai that same year. His academic career progressed in the same way. Before he departed for Egypt the second time, he was reappointed a professor, but only an honorary professor without a chair or a vote in the faculty, and once more contrary to the latter's wishes. After all, Tischendorf had never yet delivered a single lecture. He needed the professorial title primarily for purposes of prestige on his travels.

To ensure that he did not, after his third return home, bear the Codex Sinaiticus off to St Petersburg, where he had been offered a well-paid professorship, he was – once again, from above – appointed a full professor, but he still had no seat in the faculty and did not show his face there, being busy with the publication of the Codex Sinaiticus. It was not until 1 October 1867 that a 7th full professorship of biblical palaeography was created for his benefit in the theological faculty of Leipzig University, complete with all rights and obligations where research and teaching were concerned. Tischendorf was 52 years old when he embarked on regular tutorial activities at the university, where he also had to minister to students and supervise examinations. By that time he had only seven more years to live.

Tischendorf might perhaps have forgone this appointment in order to be able to pursue his real interests undisturbed, but he was financially dependent on it. Although he had been ennobled by the Tsar after the publication of the Codex Sinaiticus and could henceforth call himself Constantin *von* Tischendorf, the title brought no money. His lifelong fight for financial support continued to preoccupy him even after his great success. Instead of giving him a generous gratuity, the Tsar rewarded him for his work with 100 copies of the luxury edition of the Codex Sinaiticus, which he was supposed to sell on his own account. He described his dilemma in a letter to the Russian ministry of education in February 1864. He had, he informed

IN THE BEGINNING WAS THE WORD

his patrons in St Petersburg, *made a contract with the Leipzig firm, Fleissiger* and sold them the hundred copies. For these he had been going to receive a total of 16,000 thalers: 10,000 by the end of 1863 and the balance by May 1864. However, these payments were dependent on at least 55 copies of the codex being sold.

But business was poor and the expensive luxury editions remained unsold. The firm of Friedrich Fleissiger could not dispose of the volumes because Tsar Alexander II had already distributed free copies throughout Europe on a lavish scale. For the greater glory of imperial Russia, copies of the Codex Sinaiticus Petropolitanus had been dispatched to fellow monarchs, important persons, and major libraries. Consequently, Tischendorf requested the Russian government to take back 60 of his hundred copies and send him, in lieu of them, either 9,000 roubles or 1,200 roubles a year for ten years.

No matter how generously he was showered with honours, orders and cordial words by the mighty of his day, he still had to grub for his money, so he was glad, in the long run, that his professorship brought him a regular income. After all, he had a wife and eight children to support. However, the fact that he so obviously employed the university as a means to an end did not make him very popular with many of his colleagues.

Tischendorf and the Evangelical Alliance

This was borne in on Tischendorf when his personal involvement in a politico-religious venture ended in ignominious failure. In addition to his memberships of various associations such as the Christliche Sozietät in Berlin, the Institut d'Afrique in Paris and the Egyptian Institute in Alexandria, he also joined the ultra-conservative Evangelical Alliance, a worldwide association which may be described as a precursor of today's evangelical churches. Founded in Scotland in 1846, the Evangelical Alliance quickly spread to all Protestant countries. It was, as Tischendorf put it, *an association of evangelical, fundamentalist Christians intended to constitute a unity of the Protestant Church, as opposed to the Roman Catholic, unaffected by differences in denomination and nationality.*[10]

One of the Evangelical Alliance's principal concerns during the 1870s was to support the Protestants in Russia, whom they considered to be oppressed. In an article for the *Augsburger Allgemeine*, Tischendorf wrote that some *100,000 souls* who had been *illegally induced to go over to the Greek Church* were now having the utmost difficulty in reverting to their traditional faith.

It is clear that during the first half of the 19th century the Russian Orthodox national church had stepped up its pressure on Christians of other denominations to convert to Orthodoxy. This the Evangelical Alliance sought to combat. It had already tried to bring its influence to bear by writing and sending a small delegation to Russia, but with limited success. In 1871, therefore, a large delegation was dispatched to St Petersburg, only to be redirected to Germany, where the Tsar was spending his summer holiday.

The delegates who arrived in Friedrichshafen on Lake Constance in July 1871 and requested an audience naturally included the professor from Leipzig. Recently ennobled by the Tsar, Constantin von Tischendorf believed he could exploit his good contacts with the imperial court to further the cause – and, of course, boost his own prestige. Court circles had already intimated that the Tsar and his closest advisers were annoyed by the Evangelical Alliance's incessant démarches and regarded them as unacceptable interference in Russia's internal affairs. And so, without seeking his colleagues' consent, Tischendorf obtained a preliminary meeting with Grand Duke Constantine, the Tsar's brother and his erstwhile supporter at court. But Constantine was angry that Tischendorf should be taking part in a campaign the Tsar found so irksome and dismissed him somewhat brusquely. The Tsar then officially let it be known that the delegates should present their request to Chancellor Gorchakov, who fobbed off the Protestants with a few noncommittal remarks.

What was initially a diplomatic failure, developed, from Tischendorf's point of view, into a personal disaster that overshadowed the last few years of his life. A retired Swiss colonel named Ludwig von Wurstemberger, who had been one of the Evangelical Alliance's delegates in Friedrichshafen, accused Tischendorf of personal responsibility for the failure of the mission because, instead of representing the Protestants' interests, he had ingratiated himself with the court and betrayed his coreligionists. In 1872 Wurstemberger published a book, *Die Gewissensfreiheit in den Ostseeprovinzen Russlands* [Freedom of Conscience in the Baltic Provinces of Russia], in which he castigated Tischendorf for conducting a conversation with Grand Duke Constantine in the absence of the other delegates and accused him of sabotaging the Evangelical Alliance's request for his own benefit. But Wurstemberger's attack on Tischendorf did not become truly dangerous until it was avidly picked up in Leipzig. In an article that appeared in the *Hamburger Correspondent* in October 1872, an anonymous Leipzig colleague vented his clearly long-pent-up anger on Tischendorf.

In conclusion, the author of the article stated: 'Herr Tischendorf has never been accounted an exemplary character by his colleagues and the public of Leipzig: because of his immeasurable conceit, his tendency to self-advertisement, and his servility towards royalty and those whom he considers persons of distinction, the publisher of the Codex Sinaiticus has long played the role of a comic figure in the eyes of our society. However, the said theologian has not hitherto been accused of downright despicable behaviour and betrayal of his own church. The charges levelled in Wurstemberger's book are, in my estimation, so grave that neither the accused nor his colleagues can remain silent about them. The lack of dignity displayed by German scholars had long been an object of derision among foreigners, and nothing was able to be done about it. That a German theologian should be accused of ignominiously harming the interests of his own church and voluntarily undertaking espionage duties against the same, and that no one should comment on the fact – at least since the resurrection of the German Empire – is quite unprecedented.'[11]

Tischendorf was profoundly hurt by this defamatory campaign against him. He sued Wurstemberger and defended himself with a pamphlet of his own in which he presented a detailed account of the delegation's trip as seen from his point of view. Wurstemberger persisted in his campaign, however. He was not the cause of the anger felt by at least some of Tischendorf's colleagues, only the occasion for making their annoyance public.

This extremely hurtful dispute, coupled with overwork caused by his unremitting editorial activities and university commitments, led on 5 May 1873 to Tischendorf's suffering a stroke from which he never recovered. Despite various cures and exercises designed to help him regain the ability to speak, walk and write, he remained a sick man. On 7 December 1874, 18 months after his first stroke, which was followed by others, he died in Leipzig at the age of 59. Tischendorf left behind eight children of whom the youngest was only seven. Friends from Glasgow purchased his library, not least in order to provide his widow with some financial support.

The dispute with his coreligionists from the Evangelical Alliance, which blighted his latter years, was absurd because the charges against him were wholly unfounded. Tischendorf was undoubtedly vain and fond of hogging the limelight, and he did serve various kings and tsars during his lifetime, but he certainly never betrayed his church and his theological convictions.

Despite his research, and despite his knowledge of the apocryphal texts and of the historical fortuities to which the Bible owes its composition, Tischendorf was a fundamentalist Christian who believed every line of the Holy Scriptures to be God-given. As such, he was quite properly one of the earliest prominent members of the Evangelical Alliance, still the world's oldest international Protestant organization, which campaigns in favour of the literal truth of the Bible and against the secularization of society. More than one million people belong to it in Germany alone. The German Evangelical Alliance consists of private individuals and regards itself as a network of conservative Christians. According to its own figures, it is in contact with 342 organizations worldwide, and maintains 1,105 centres and meeting places inside Germany alone. Its magazine, *EiNS*, appears quarterly and reports on the work of the organization.[12] The spirit prevailing within the Evangelical Alliance and its fundamentalist view of the Bible are also a legacy from Constantin von Tischendorf.

The Church of the Divine Wisdom

Like Rome, the historic Old City of Istanbul, formerly known as Constantinople and Byzantium, is dominated by seven hills. The big sultanic mosques whose minarets are so characteristic of Istanbul's

skyline stand on all but one of them. Presiding over the most important hill, the one immediately beyond the palace on the tip of the peninsula, is Hagia Sophia, the Church of the Divine Wisdom, ('Megale
Ekklesia' or 'Big Church' in Greek). Its dome, which is 56 metres
high, still dominates the city's former imperial precinct. The palace
of the Ottoman sultans, from which a world empire was ruled for 500
years, is eclipsed by Hagia Sophia, and even the famous Blue Mosque,
built to rival Hagia Sophia, cannot outshine it despite its size and six
minarets. Although the height of the dome was a unique architectural achievement at the time the church was built, the building looks
squat rather than towering from the outside. 'It crouches on top of the
city like a tortoise,' as one 19th-century traveller aptly put it.

Orders for the building of Hagia Sophia were issued by Justinian,
the Byzantine emperor who also decreed in favour of the construc-
tion of St Catherine's Monastery in the Sinai Desert. Although Hagia
Sophia was consecrated as an imperial cathedral in 537 and the desert
monastery was not completed until 30 years later, both buildings are
products and manifestations of the heyday of the Byzantine Empire.
Byzantium was never greater or more powerful than under Emperor
Justinian, but the histories of these two cultural monuments have been
very different. St Catherine's Monastery, already on the periphery of
the empire when it was built, almost disappeared from the perceptions
of the outside world for 1,500 years and has remained, as if enclosed in
a time capsule, a faithful reflection of the life of its founding fathers.

Hagia Sophia's fate has followed quite another course, as even a first
fleeting glance makes clear. The dome of what was once the biggest
and most important church in Christendom is today flanked by four
minarets. On the south side are five mausoleums in which sultans'
whole families lie in state. When entering the building through
the big portal originally reserved for the emperor, one is met by a
remarkable sight. At the other end of the huge interior space, above
which the dome seems to float, freely suspended, is the place where
the altar used to be. This is now occupied by a prayer niche, or so-
called *mihrab*, which faces Mecca as in every mosque. On the corner
columns of the dome hang big, oval wooden plaques bearing, in
Arabic script, the names of Allah, Mohammed, the first four caliphs,
and the Prophet's two grandsons, Hassan and Hussain. Resplendent

beside these, however, are four angels – the face of one of them was recently restored – and in the apse, on the dome over the chancel, gleams a mosaic, underlaid with gold, of Mary with Jesus on her lap.

The whole building is full of surprises in the realm of cultural history. For example, although several mosaics depict Byzantine emperors engaging in religious activities, there are no imperial tombs in the former cathedral. On the other hand, buried in the upper eastern gallery are the remains of the Venetian doge Enrico Dandolo, the man who, as leader of the Fourth Crusade, was responsible for the destruction of Constantinople and represents the victory of the Latin Catholic Church over Orthodox Byzantium.

Today, the former Church of the Divine Wisdom is truly an expression of wisdom. It symbolizes the overcoming of once deadly antitheses and their remodelling into a new architectural ensemble. The centre of Christendom for almost a millennium, the building then became the central mosque of the Ottoman Empire and was ultimately, in keeping with the ethos of the secular Turkish Republic, transformed into a museum in 1934. Hagia Sophia has thus become a unique cultural monument in a part of the world moulded by Greek antiquity, Christianity and Islam. All can visit it, no one is excluded.

The history of Hagia Sophia goes as far back as that of the Codex Sinaiticus and St Catherine's Monastery. The Church of the Divine Wisdom has become a religio-historical museum, and the Codex Sinaiticus, at least since it has been on the Internet, has mutated into a document relating to cultural history. Only the monastery in the desert continues to defy the modern age. The life of the monks has scarcely changed with the coming of cars and planes, television and telephone. The rules established 1,500 years ago still prevail behind their lofty walls. The world into which those men have withdrawn is a world all its own. It is a hard world for outsiders to comprehend and almost impossible to live in for any length of time. Although the spirituality of the place can exert a great fascination on non-believers as well, the monks' rejection of the reality outside their walls creates an insurmountable gulf between us. My stay in their world left a lasting impression on me, but I was glad to return to the modern age. Even Cairo, the city that had thoroughly bewildered me two weeks earlier, now seemed like familiar territory, and Istanbul felt like home.

Appendix

Constantin von Tischendorf's Life

Constantin Tischendorf is born on **18 January 1815** at Lengenfeld in the Vogtland (Saxony).

His father works as a forensic physician in Lengenfeld.

In **1829**, after attending primary school in Lengenfeld, he moves on to the grammar school in Plauen.

At Easter **1834**, having left school with excellent marks, he proceeds to study theology and philosophy at Leipzig University.

In **1835** his father dies, followed only a year later by his mother.

In **1838**, despite this, Tischendorf gains his doctorate of philosophy. Immediately afterwards he takes a tutoring job in Grossstädeln, where he lives in the home of the Reverend Ferdinand Leberecht Zehme. There he meets and falls in love with Angelika Zehme, the clergyman's daughter and his wife-to-be.

In **1838** and **1839**, Tischendorf tries his hand as a poet and author. He publishes a volume of poetry entitled *Maiknospen* [Buds of May] and, under a pseudonym, *Der junge Mystiker* [The Young Mystic].

In **1839**, while working as a tutor, Tischendorf embarks on a first critical edition of the New Testament in Greek, thereby finding his life's vocation at an early stage.

On **26 October 1840** Tischendorf habilitates with the foreword to his edition of the Greek Bible, which qualifies him to give lectures at the university. Instead of making use of this right, however, he leaves only four days later, on **30 October 1840**, for Paris, where he works on deciphering the Codex Ephraemi.

In **1843** and **1845** his edition of the Codex Ephraemi is published in Leipzig by Bernhard Tauchnitz Jun. This lays the foundations of his extraordinary reputation as a palaeographer.

In November **1843** Tischendorf receives word that the Saxon ministry of culture and science is prepared to sponsor an expedition to the East to the tune of 1,000 thalers. Thanks to further private contributions and the income from his publications, Tischendorf can now make ready for his first expedition to the sources of the Bible.

In **March 1844** he sets off on his first trip to Egypt.

In **May 1844** he leaves Cairo on his first expedition to St Catherine's Monastery in Sinai. There his discovers the first 129 parchment leaves of what subsequently becomes known as the **Codex Sinaiticus**. He contrives to take 43 of those sheets back to Leipzig with him.

In **January 1845** he returns to Leipzig and is appointed an extraordinary professor of philosophy.

On **18 September 1845** Tischendorf marries Angelika Zehme.

In **1846** he publishes his discovery in Leipzig under the title *Codex Friderico-Augustanus*.

Between **1847** and **1858** the children Paul, Johannes, Konstanze, Immanuel and Angelika are born. Another four siblings follow later.

In **1850** Tischendorf is appointed an honorary professor and delivers occasional lectures.

In **1853**, however, he leaves the university behind once more and sets off on his second trip to the East, again with financial backing from the court of Saxony. The expedition proves a great disappointment because he never gets to see the 86 pages of the **Codex Sinaiticus** still at the monastery. He is back in Leipzig after barely four months.

In **November 1858**, after lengthy spadework, Tischendorf secures permission from the Tsarist court in Russia to equip himself for a third expedition to Egypt and to travel there on the Tsar's behalf.

In **January 1859** Tischendorf sets off on his third and last expedition to the East.

His great day dawns on **4 February 1859**. At the Sinai monastery, Tischendorf gets hold of 346 parchment sheets bearing large parts of the **Old Testament** and a complete version of the **New Testament** written in old Greek uncial script. He has laid hands on the earliest extant version of the New Testament, a find that goes down in history as the **Codex Sinaiticus**.

Back in Cairo on **24 February 1859,** Tischendorf begins copying the codex.

On **9 October 1859**, having borrowed his find from the monks, he sets sail for Europe. In St Petersburg on **19 November 1859** he presents the original manuscript to the Tsar.

On **1 October 1867** Tischendorf finally obtains a full chair of biblical palaeography.

Negotiations over the donation of the Codex Sinaiticus drag on for ten years. In **1869** the archbishop finally approves it. In the same year Tischendorf is ennobled by the Tsar and becomes Constantin *von* Tischendorf.

In **1872** he completes his last edition of the Greek New Testament.

On **5 May 1873** Tischendorf suffers a stroke – the first of several – from which he never recovers.

He dies in Leipzig on **7 December 1874**, at the age of only 59.

Notes

The Desert Monastery (pp. 1–15)

1 The Sinai Peninsula lies between Egypt and Israel like a natural buffer. After nationalizing the Suez Canal, President Nasser declared it a demilitarized zone in which UN troops were temporarily stationed. From May 1967 onwards, after they were withdrawn at Nasser's request, Egypt deployed troops in Sinai.

The Israelis construed this as a *casus belli*, and on 5 June 1967 they launched surprise air raids on all Egypt's military airfields, almost annihilating the Egyptian air force. They then launched their invasion of Sinai, which culminated in total victory on the banks of the Suez Canal.

Israeli troops occupied the peninsula for 11 years until, in September 1978, President Jimmy Carter helped to negotiate the Camp David Accords between Israel and Egypt. President Anwar al-Sadat of Egypt and the Israeli premier Menachem Begin concluded a peace treaty which stipulated, among other things, that Israeli troops should withdraw from Sinai. Although other parts of the treaty were never honoured, Israeli troops did in fact withdraw from Sinai. By April 1982 the peninsula had been completely vacated and reoccupied by Egypt.

2 During the celebrated first Council of Nicaea, convoked in 325 by Emperor Constantine in order to unify Christendom and establish a binding doctrine at last, Alexandria was described as a patriarchate that took precedence over Rome, Constantinople and Antioch. The schism occurred in 451, 125 years later, at the Council of Chalcedon. The reason for the schism was the everlasting debate

over 'the nature of Christ'. The Council of Nicaea had been convoked mainly to resolve this controversy. Back then it was initially the followers of the presbyter Arius who threatened the unity of the Church. Arius regarded Jesus primarily as a man who was later taken up into heaven by God, so the object was to convince Arius that Jesus was divine in nature from the outset. The same point was at issue at Chalcedon 125 years later, but by this time the majority tended to describe Jesus as God as well as man. The majority of Alexandrian Christians refused to accept this. 'We shall abide by the resolutions of Nicaea,' Patriarch Dioscorus of Alexandria insisted after the council ended.

The majority at Chalcedon accepted the formula 'Christ is the only begotten Son and Lord, to be acknowledged in two natures, inconfusedly, unchangeably, indivisibly, inseparably', whereas the delegates from Alexandria insisted that Jesus had a simultaneously divine and human nature that was as unified as fire and iron in a piece of red-hot iron. That marked the birth of the independent Coptic Church.

Those who fail to spot any great difference between these formulas, and cannot, even after consulting specialized theological literature, understand why one or the other should have caused a final rift, need not doubt their own intelligence. In 1988, a good 1,500 years later, Pope John Paul II and the Coptic Pope Shenouda III agreed that it had all been a mere misunderstanding occasioned by the difficulty of the Greek language, and may also have had political causes.

It must, in fact, be assumed that the true reason for the schism was power politics rather than theological hair-splitting. As already mentioned, the patriarchates of Alexandria and Antioch were Christianity's original heavyweights. Although Rome already played an important role in the 2nd century, the disputes at the four councils up to Chalcedon in 451 made it very clear that the impulses emanated from Alexandria and amounted more and more to a conflict with Constantinople, while Rome did not play a decisive role until Chalcedon. The role of Alexandria was gradually eroded by the founding of Constantinople in 330 and its elevation of Christianity to the state religion of Rome. Alexandria's secession after the council of 451 was also an acknowledgement of Constantinople's by now incontestable position of power, to which Alexandria was unwilling to subordinate itself. The Egyptian and Syrian churches, in other words, Alexandria and Antioch, thereupon separated from Constantinople, whose own split with Rome did not occur for another 500 years.

Constantine the Founder (pp. 16–27)

1 See Clauss, Manfred: *Konstantin der Grosse und seine Zeit*. Clauss briefly examines various historical assessments. One of them, which portrays Constantine mainly from a Christian point of view, is that of Hermann Dörries in his *Konstantin der Grosse*.

2 Constantine's career is interpreted in accordance with the latest historical findings in Hartwin Brandt's *Konstantin der Grosse* of 2006. Although Brandt cites many examples which make it clear that Constantine granted the Christian religion more and more privileges in the course of his career, not even Brandt can explain exactly why the Roman general should have behaved in this way.

3 The marble head and other fragments of the only surviving colossal statue of Constantine were found near the Basilica of Constantine in Rome in 1486. They can now be seen in Rome's *Musei Capitolini*.

In 2007 the city of Trier mounted an extensive Constantine exhibition including the famous head. Published to accompany it was a very informative catalogue (Demandt and Engemann (eds): 'Konstantin der Grosse', Trier, 2007).

4 See the section on the canonization of the New Testament in the chapter 'In the Beginning Was the Word'.

5 See also the chapter 'The Book of Books' on the history of the Codex Sinaiticus.

6 John Julius Norwich's *Byzantium: The Decline and Fall* is particularly informative in this respect.

The Obsessive (pp. 28–43)

1 Tischendorf: *Reise in den Orient*. The page numbers refer to an English translation of the above originally published in 1847 under the title *Travels in the East*, of which a facsimile edition was published by Cambridge University Press in 2010. However, W E Shuckard's 1847 version has been extensively modified by the present translator for accuracy and readability's sake.

2 Tischendorf: *Travels in the East*, pp. 23–4.

3 Ibid, pp. 23–5.

4 Albert Schweitzer, known to most readers primarily as a 'jungle doctor' and Nobel Peace Prize laureate, was also one of the leading theologians of the first half of the 20th century. His most important theological work is *The Quest of the Historical Jesus*, now in its 9th, expanded, edition.

5 Ludwig Schneller: *Tischendorf-Erinnerungen*, p. 10 f.

6 Hildegard Behrend is Constantin Tischendorf's granddaughter, the daughter of his second-youngest daughter, Elisabeth Behrend. In 1952 she published a pamphlet about her grandfather, *Auf der Suche nach Schätzen* [In Search of Treasures]. This pamphlet aroused great interest, according to her, so she developed it into a small research project of her own which kept on appearing in new and expanded editions. By the time the 10th edition came out in 1969, still entitled *Auf der Suche nach Schätzen*, it was a proper little book.

   In her foreword to the 10th edition, Hildegard Behrend wrote that her most important source had been the letters from Tischendorf to her mother, his wife Angelika, which she had preserved. Hildegard also thanked her mother for having transcribed Tischendorf's letters, which were very hard to decipher, thereby enabling her to read their correspondence.

7 Quoted from 'Zur Kritik des Neuen Testaments', an essay in which Tischendorf reviewed and classified his work prior to his first trip to the East, in Christfried Böttrich (ed.): *Tischendorf-Lesebuch. Bibelforschung in Reiseabenteuern*, Leipzig, 1999. Apart from Tischendorf's own works and books by members of his family, this collection of his letters and essays was one of my most important

sources. Just as Hildegard Behrend could have recourse to her mother's transcripts of his correspondence, so Christfried Böttrich's selection and editing of his letters and essays was of invaluable assistance to me.

8 Tischendorf: 'Zur Kritik des Neuen Testaments'. Ibid.

9 From an account by Tischendorf of his audience with Pope Gregory XVI on 21 May 1843. In Böttrich: *Tischendorf-Lesebuch*, p. 74.

10 Tishcendorf: 'Rückblick auf Pariser Unternehmungen'. In Böttrich, *Tishcendorf-Lesebuch*, p. 74.

11 Behrend: *Suche nach Schätzen*, p. 18, which also includes the quotation that follows.

12 The quotations are from a letter written by Tischendorf to his brother on the eve of his departure for Alexandria on 12 March 1844. In Böttrich, *Tischendorf-Lesebuch*, p. 89 f.

13 Tischendorf: *Travels in the East*, p. 9.

The Last Byzantines (pp. 45–62)

1 An introduction to the peculiarities and structures of the Orthodox Churches can be found in Johannes Oeldemann: *Die Kirchen des christlichen Ostens*, Regensburg, 2006. Petros A Botsis is informative about the nature of Orthodoxy in *Was ist Orthodoxie?*, Athens, 1981.

2 On questions to do with the layout and functioning of Orthodox churches, see also John Chryssavgis: *The Ecumenical Patriarchate. A Historical Guide*, Ecumenical Patriarchate Publications, Istanbul, 2006.

3 The structure of the monastery is illustrated with particular clarity by John Galey's photographs in *Das Katharinenkloster auf dem Sinai*, Belser Verlag, Stuttgart/Zurich, 1997.

4 Quoted from Kurt Weitzmann: 'Zur Geschichte des Katharinenklosters' in Galey: *Das Katharinenkloster auf dem Sinai*, p. 12.

Through the Desert (pp. 63–80)

1 Tischendorf: *Travels in the East*, pp. 89–90.
2 Böttrich: *Tischendorf-Lesebuch*, p. 93.
3 Tischendorf: *Travels in the East*, p. 71.
4 Ibid., p. 72.
5 Gerhard Prause: 'Auf den Spuren der Ramsesstadt', in *Die Zeit*, 17 February 1984.
6 Tischendorf: *Travels in the East*, pp. 74 and 80.
7 Ibid., p. 82.
8 Ibid. pp. 87–8.
9 Ibid., pp. 88–9.
10 Ibid., pp. 94–5.
11 Böttrich: *Tischendorf-Lesebuch*, p. 93.
12 Tischendorf: *Travels in the East*, p. 95.
13 Ibid., pp. 31–2.
14 Ibid., p. 29.
15 Ibid. p. 50.
16 Ibid., p. 30.
17 Ibid. p. 52.
18 Ibid.

The Sacred Mountain (pp. 81–90)

1 Tischendorf: *Travels in the East*, pp. 100–1.
2 Ibid., pp. 95–6.
3 Ibid., p. 99.
4 Ibid., pp. 99–100.

The Discovery (pp. 91–111)

1 Böttrich: *Tischendorf-Lesebuch*, p. 103.
2 Tischendorf: *Die-Sinaibibel*, p. 3 f.
3 Böttrich: *Tischendorf-Lesebuch*, p. 95.
4 Ibid., pp. 111 f.

5 Ibid., p. 124.
6 Ibid., p. 131.
7 Tischendorf: *Die Sinaibibel*, p. 5.
8 Ibid., p. 5 f.
9 Ibid., p. 6.
10 Ibid., p. 7.
11 Ibid., p. 10.
12 Böttrich: *Tischendorf-Lesebuch*, p. 169.
13 Ibid., p. 170.
14 Ibid., p. 171.
15 Ibid.
16 Tischendorf: *Die Sinaibibel*, p. 12.
17 Ibid., p. 13, where also the quotation that follows.
18 Böttrich: *Tischendorf-Lesebuch*, p. 172.
19 Tischendorf: *Die Sinaibibel*, p. 16.

In the Tsar's Service (pp. 112–128)

1 Tischendorf: *Die Sinaibibel*, p. 16.
2 Tischendorf's letter to the grand duke forms part of his literary remains in Leipzig University Library, where I was able to examine it.
3 Tischendorf: *Die Sinaibibel*, p. 22.
4 Böttrich: *Tischendorf-Lesebuch*, p. 210.
5 Ibid., p. 211. Source: Kurt Aland: 'Konstantin von Tischendorf (1815–1874). Neutestamentliche Textforschung damals und heute' (minutes of the Saxon Academy of Sciences), Berlin, 1993. The text is there reproduced in Greek with an English translation; the receipt was also displayed for years in the Sinai monastery to demonstrate that Tischendorf had undertaken to return the Codex.
6 Tischendorf: *Die Sinaibibel*, p. 26 f.
7 Porfiry Uspensky: 'Opinion on the Bible Manuscript of Sinai', no place or date.
8 Tischendorf: *Die Sinaibibel*, p. 55 f.
9 Ibid., p. 39.
10 Ibid., p. 89.
11 Nicolas Fyssas presented this correspondence in a lecture on the

Codex Sinaiticus delivered at a conference held by the British Library on 6 and 7 July 2009. The conference transcripts have not yet been published.

12 In 2005, Professor Böttrich published a detailed analysis of the tortuous route followed by the 'donation' of the Codex Sinaiticus to the Tsar of Russia. Christfried Böttrich: 'Constantin von Tischendorf und der Transfer des Codex Sinaiticus nach St. Petersburg', in Andreas Gössner, (ed.): *Die Theologische Fakultät der Universität Leipzig. Personen, Profile und Perspektiven aus sechs Jahrhunderten Fakultätsgeschichte*, Leipzig, 2005. pp. 253–7. Leipzig University Library also proposed that Professor Böttrich write a historical essay on the 'donation' for publication on the website of the Codex Sinaiticus project. This idea was eventually dropped because of objections from the Sinai monks, but the essay will shortly appear in book form.

The Book of Books (pp. 129–146)

1 The British Library's conference on the Codex Sinaiticus was held in London on 6 and 7 July 2009. Taking part were the four institutions that now hold parts of the Codex; that is to say, in addition to the British Library itself, Leipzig University Library, the National Library of St Petersburg, and St Catherine's Monastery in Sinai. Also participating in the conference were nearly all the world's experts on the history of Christian codices dating from the early centuries AD.

2 See also Orlando Figes: *A People's Tragedy. The Russian Revolution 1891–1924*.

3 Waltraut Bayer (ed.): *Verkaufte Kultur. Die sowjetische Kunst und Antiquitätenexporte 1919–1938*. Frankfurt am Main, 2001.

4 Cf. Leipzig University (ed.): *Codex Sinaiticus. Geschichte und Erschliessung der 'Sinai-Bible'*. Leipzig, 2007.

5 Philip Howard: *The British Library. A Treasure House of Knowledge*. Scala Publishers, London, 2008.

6 Cf. Leipzig University Library (ed.): *Codex Sinaiticus*.

7 Ulrich Johannes Schneider: 'Die Kraft einer Handschrift. Der

Codex Sinaiticus im Internet' in *Bibliotheken in Sachsen*, vol. 3 (2008), pp. 154–7.

8 www.codexsinaiticus.net. The English text can be found under 'History'.

In the Beginning Was the Word (pp. 147–164)

1 Tischendorf: *Die Sinaibibel*, p. 1 f.

2 Ibid, p. 81 f.

3 Ibid, p. 82.

4 The Epistle of Barnabas, which in the Codex Sinaiticus still forms part of the New Testament, contains a quotation from St Matthew's Gospel. In this, the phrase 'as it is written' appears. According to Tischendorf, this form of words was not used in the gospels until they were placed on a par with the Old Testament, in other words, recognized as sacred canonical texts. Since the Epistle of Barnabas was written around AD 120, Tischendorf infers that St Matthew's Gospel was already a generally accepted part of the New Testament by this time.

5 Gerd Theissen is Professor of New Testament Theology at Heidelberg University. He has devoted himself both theologically and belletristically to the early history of Christianity, the canonization of the New Testament, and the historical Jesus. I have derived valuable ideas from the following books by him: *Der historische Jesus. Ein Lehrbuch*; *Der Schatten des Galiläers*; *Die Entstehung des Neuen Testaments als literaturgeschichtliches Problem*.

6 Katharina Ceming is a philosopher and lecturer in theology at Augsburg University. Jürgen Werlitz is a professor, likewise at Augsburg University. In their foreword to the 2nd edition they say how surprised they were by the great interest the book aroused. They conclude that the apocryphal texts and, thus, the question of the Bible's canonization are currently being discussed with renewed attention.

7 It is apparent from the three synoptic gospels (Mark, Matthew and Luke) that Matthew and Luke adopted a large proportion of Mark's material, but that they also quote sayings from Jesus of which Mark

was ignorant. The inference is that they had access to a written collection of sayings unavailable to Mark. Although no such collection has ever been found, its existence has been rendered more likely by the discovery in 1945 at Nag Hammadi in Upper Egypt, because its apocryphal Gospel of Thomas is based on the same collection of sayings. This so-called 'Q Source' was probably translated into Greek from an original Aramaic text which probably hailed from the Palestine area and was written in AD 40–50.

8 Gerd Theissen: *Die Entstehung des Neuen Testaments als literaturgeschichtliches Problem*. Universitätsverlag Winter, Heidelberg 2007, p. 292. The theologian David J Trobisch, who teaches at American and German universities and is one of Tischendorf's best-known successors as a palaeographer, even assumes that Bishop Polycarp of Smyrna put together a first version of the New Testament in around AD 170.

9 Gerd Theissen: *Die Entstehung des Neuen Testaments als literaturgeschichtliches Problem*. Universitätsverlag Winter, Heidelberg, 2007, p. 322. In her book *Beyond Belief. The Secret Gospel of Thomas*, Elaine H Pagels explores the question of whether the church's decision to exclude this so-called Gospel of Thomas from the canon robbed the Bible of a whole dimension of spiritual strength. Having jointly worked on the publication of the apocryphal texts found at Nag Hammadi, she believes that the outlawing of the Gospel of Thomas as a gnostic deviation was wrong.

10 Böttrich: *Tischendorf-Lesebuch*, p. 266 f.

11 From Tischendorf's papers in Leipzig University Library.

12 See the website of the Evangelical Alliance: www.eauk.org

Bibliography

Constantin von Tischendorf

Travels in the East. W. E. Shuckard's translation of *Reise in den Orient*, Leipzig, 1846. Facsimile edition published in 2010 by Cambridge University Press.

Die Anfechtungen der Sinai-Bible. Verlag Carl Fr. Fleische, Leipzig, 1863.

Die Sinaibibel. Ihre Entdeckung, Herausgabe und Erwerbung. Giesecke & Devrient, Leipzig, 1871. New edition: Schick, Alexander (ed.): *Die Sinaibibel (Reprint). Ihre Entdeckung, Herausgabe und Erwerbung,* with an explanatory commentary by A. Schick. Hammerbrücke, 2010.

Biographical works about Tischendorf

Aland, Kurt: *Konstantin von Tischendorf (1815–1874). Neutestamentliche Textforschung damals und heute.* Akademie-Verlag, Berlin 1993.

Behrend, Hildegard: *Auf der Suche nach Schätzen.* EVA, 10th edition, Berlin, 1970.

Böttrich, Christfried (ed.): *Tischendorf-Lesebuch. Bibelforchung in Reiseabenteuern.* EVA, Leipzig, 1999.

Konstantin Tischendorf. Eine Bibliographie. Universitätsverlag, Leipzig, 1999.

Schliesske, Otto: *Der Schatz im Wüstenkloster.* Memra Verlag, Neuwied, 1983.

Schneller, Ludwig: *Tischendorf-Erinnerungen.* Verlag der St.-Johannis-Druckerei, Lahr, 1954, most recently Verlag C. Schweickhardt, Lahr, 1991.

History

Assmann, Jan: *Die Mosaische Unterscheidung.* Carl Hanser Verlag, Munich, 2003.
Cinok, Fatih: *Das biblische Anatolien. Von der Genesis bis zu den Konzilen.* Tourizm Yayinlar, Istanbul, 2005.
Figes, Orlando: *A People's Tragedy. The Russian Revolution 1891–1924.* Jonathan Cape, London, 1996.
Galey, John: *Sinai and the Monastery of St Catherine.* Doubleday, New York, 1980.
Gibbon, Edward: *The History of the Decline and Fall of the Roman Empire.* Penguin Books, London, 2000.
Josephus, Flavius: *The Jewish War.* Penguin Books, London, 1981.
Müller-Wiener, Wolfgang: *Die historische Topographie Istanbuls.* Wasmuth Verlag, Tübingen, 1977.
Stoll. Heinrich Alexander: *Die Höhle am Toten Meer.* Verlag Werner Dausien, Hanau, 1962.

Byzantium and Emperor Constantine

Brandt, Hartwin: *Konstantin der Grosse. Der erste christliche Kaiser.* C. H. Beck Verlag, Munich, 2nd ed. 2007.
Chryssavgis, John: *The Ecumenical Patriarchate. A Historical Guide.* Ecumenical Patriarchate Publications, Istanbul, 2006.
Clauss, Manfred: *Konstantin der Grosse und seine Zeit.* C. H. Beck Verlag, Munich, 1996.
Demandt, Alexander; Engemann, Josef (eds): 'Konstantin der Grosse. Imperator Caesar Flavius Constantinus' (exhibition catalogue). Von Zabern Verlag, Trier, 2007.
Dörries, Hermann: *Konstantin der Grosse.* Kohlhammer Verlag, Stuttgart, 1958.

Ducellier, Alain: *Byzanz. Das Reich und die Stadt.* Campus Verlag, Frankfurt am Main, 1990.

Meier, Mischa: *Justinian. Herrschaft, Reich und Religion.* C. H. Beck Verlag, Munich, 2004.

Norwich, John J.: *Byzantium: The Decline and Fall.* Viking, London, 1995.

Oeldemann, Johannes: *Die Kirchen des christlichen Ostens.* Regensburg, 2006.

The Bible

Böttrich, Christfried: 'Das Dossier des russischen Ministers Golovnin von 1862 zur Frage des "Codex Sinaiticus"' in *Scriptorium* (Brussels) 63/2, 2009, pp. 288–326.

Stuttgart Jubilee Bible with explanatory notes. Privileg. Württembergische Bibelanstalt, Stuttgart, 1949.

Leipzig University Library (ed.): *Codex Sinaiticus. Geschichte und Erschliessung der 'Sinai-Bibel'*, Leipzig, 2007.

Uspensky, Porfiry: 'Meinung über das Bibel-Manuscript von Sinai.' No place or date.

Ecclesiastical History

Deschner, Karl-Heinz: *Kriminalgeschichte des Christentums.* Vol. 1, Rowohlt Verlag, 6th ed., Reinbek, 2006.

Heim, Manfred: *Kirchengeschichte in Daten.* C. H. Beck Verlag, Munich, 2006.

Küng, Hans: *Kleine Geschichte der katholischen Kirche.* Berliner Taschenbuch Verlag, Berlin, 2003.

Oeldemann, Johannes: *Die Kirchen des christlichen Ostens. Orthodoxe, orientalische und mit Rom unierte Ostkirchen.* Verlagsgemeinschaft Topos, Kevelaer, 2006.

Rosa, Peter de: *Vicars of Christ: The Dark Side of the Papacy.* Crown, London, 1998.

The Jesus Complex

Augstein, Rudolf: *Jesus Menschensohn*. Rowohlt Verlag, Reinbeck, 1974.

Cemin, Katharina; Werlitz, Jürgen: *Die Verbotenen Evangelien. Apokryphe Schriften*. Piper Verlag, Munich, 2008.

Pagels, Elaine: *Beyond Belief. The Secret Gospel of Thomas*. Vintage Books, London, 2003.

Schweitzer, Albert: *The Quest of the Historical Jesus*. Alban Books, Edinburgh, 2001.

Theissen, Gerd; Merz, Annette: *Der historische Jesus. Ein Lehrbuch*. Verlag Vandenhoeck & Ruprecht, Göttingen, 2001.

Theissen, Gerd: *Die Entstehung des Neuen Testaments als literaturgeschichtliches Problem*. Universitätsverlag Winter, Heidelberg, 2007.

Theissen, Gerd: *Der Schatten des Galiläers. Historische Jesusforschung in erzählender Form*. Gütersloher Verlagshaus, 21st ed., Gütersloh, 2008.

Verhoeven, Paul: *Jesus. Die Geschichte eines Menschen*. Piper Verlag, Munich, 2009.

Illustrations

Historical Picture Archive/CORBIS: cover image
Christopher Volle, Freiburg: p. vii
Matson (G. Eric and Edith) Photograph Collection/Library of
     Congress, Washington: pp. 2, 44, 49, 64, 74, 78, 82, 84, 88, 94
Archive of Christoph Links Verlag: pp. 14, 23, 130
Estate Ludwig Schneller by Rosmarie Siebert: reproduced courtesy
     of Orient-Bildarchiv Alexander Schick, Westerland, © www.
     bibelausstelliung.de: p. 29
Leipzig University Library, Ms gr. I, sheet 27a: p. 92 and back cover
dpa/Picture Alliance: p. 143 (no. 9200250)

Acknowledgements

In the course of researching and writing *The Bible Hunter* I came across many interested listeners and informants. I would, however, like to say a special word of thanks to the monks of St Catherine's in Sinai, but for whose hospitality I would not have become acquainted with life in their monastery and could not have written this book, at least in its present form. The same goes for Professor Dr Ulrich Johannes Schneider, director of Leipzig University Library, and his colleagues in the library's Special Collection. With their permission and assistance I was able to peruse Tischendorf's literary estate and study his books and essays. I also owe a special debt of gratitude to Professor Christfried Böttrich. Not only did his *Tischendorf-Lesebuch* greatly facilitate my research, but he gave me valuable hints in the course of several conversations and preserved me from many an error by looking through the manuscript.

Last but not least, my thanks go to Michael Sontheimer and Christian Semler for their suggestions and for also looking through the manuscript, likewise to my wife Dilek for her moral and intellectual support for the project.

Jürgen Gottschlich